BAPTISM BY FIRE

SELECTED LETTERS AND PERSONAL ACCOUNTS
FROM THE GREAT WAR

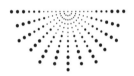

KEVIN GORMAN

SCHULMEISTER PUBLISHING LTD

CONTENTS

INTRODUCTION

"The English soldier is the best trained soldier in the world. The English soldier's fire is ten thousand times worse than hell. If we could only beat the English it would be well for us, but I am afraid we shall never be able to beat these English devils."

The above German Officer's testament [which was found in a letter] can be considered pretty accurate as the letters and personal accounts in this book demonstrate. However the contents of this book do not only give a very clear insight into the hardships, courage and sacrifices of the English soldier it also provides accounts from French, Irish and American soldiers.

It is now almost one hundred years since the end of the First World War, its importance is still very much engrained in our way of life. Every year we remember and pay our respects at Cenotaphs and memorials to the fallen around the world. Therefore, we should still strive to analyse and challenge the concepts of that war and never forget the men and woman who fought and died in a war that was supposed to have ended all wars! One way of doing this is by keeping alive the letters and personal accounts of those who were there, the witnesses of war! This book has aimed to do that!

The letters and personal accounts were selected because they reflect the author's candidness, rich historical detail in describing their situation on the battlefield. They also touch on the stress and the mental anguish of what it was like being at war. Moreover, there are glimpses of sadness in the personal undertones in the letters to a mother or a brother. Also, there are tales of selfless acts of gallantry. Lastly, there is the testament to the cruelty of being a prisoner of war! But most of all you get that sense of the will to survive on the battlefield and the Great War itself!

GREEN JACKETS IN THE FIRING LINE

Rifleman John R Brice, King's Royal Rifle Corps

*W*hen we first landed in France we were welcomed and cheered by crowds of French people who decked us with flowers and couldn't do too much for us, and they kept that kindness up all the time I was over there until I was sent home with a lot more wounded. Throwing flowers at us was a great deal pleasanter than the shells and bullets which were shot at us a few days later, when we were in the thick of trench-digging and fighting. It's astonishing how soon you settle down to a state of things that you've never been used to and how extraordinarily war alters life and people.

The Green Jackets are very proud of themselves, especially in time of peace, and have many little ways of their own; but a war like this makes all soldiers chums and equals and even the officers are practically just like the men. Our own colonel did his share in the trench-digging, and a royal officer like Prince Maurice of Battenberg, who is now resting in a soldier's grave, was living the same life as the rest of us. Many an act of kindness did the Prince show to his riflemen, and many a fierce fight he shared in before he was killed in battle; many a word of cheer did he utter to men who were almost exhausted and nearly dying of thirst, and

I have seen him go and buy fresh bread, when it could be got, and give it to us as a treat--and a glorious treat it was!

One of the first things we had to do after the retirement from Mons was to bury German dead, and you will get some idea of the awful losses they suffered, even at the beginning of the war, when I tell you that in one place alone we were about eight hours in doing this unpleasant task.

We got used to digging ourselves in and being shelled out, and to guarding towns and villages while the panic-stricken inhabitants escaped to safety. It was a pitiful sight to see people turned out of their houses, taking their belongings, when they could, in carts, perambulators, wheelbarrows and every available conveyance. They always kept as close to us as they could keep, and our fellows used to collect money amongst themselves for the poor souls and give them all the food they could spare--and they were very grateful if we gave them only a biscuit.

It was terrible work on our way to the Aisne; but the hardships were lightened for us in many little ways that counted a lot. Some of our officers would carry two rifles, when men became too weary to carry their own; the colonel would jump off his horse and give an exhausted man a lift in the saddle, and he would take apples from his pockets and pass them along the ranks to the men. These acts of kindness helped us all enormously. And we were helped on the way by smoking--what a joy it was to get a fag, especially when cigarettes ran so short that one would go round a dozen times, passed from man to man, and a chap was sorely tempted to take a pull that was almost enough to fill him with smoke. When we hadn't a scrap of tobacco of any sort we would roll a fag of dried tea-leaves which had been used for making tea--and that was better than nothing.

It was fighting all the way to the Aisne, heavy rearguard actions most of the time, though in a lesser war many of these affairs would have been reckoned proper battles. One night, at about ten o'clock, after a hard march, we had reached a town, and had thankfully gone into our billets--houses, barns, any sort of place that came handy, and we were expecting a peaceful time; but we were no sooner settling down than we got the alarm to dress and fall in. Getting dressed was the work of seconds only, because undressing was merely a case of putting the pack and equipment and rifle down and resting on the flags or earth, or, if we were lucky, hay or straw; and so, when the alarm was given, we very soon fell in, and with fixed bayonets we rushed for a bridge across the river that we had been ordered to take.

At the point of the bayonet the bridge was carried with a splendid rush, then we had to hold it while our transport and ammunition column got out of the town, and there we were till seven o'clock next morning. The main body of the troops retired and left us as a rearguard; but they had not gone from the town more than ten minutes when we saw the Germans coming towards the bridge in swarms. There was no help for it--we had to get away from the bridge which we had held throughout the night.

We began to retire in good order, fighting desperately, and our men falling killed and wounded. Yard by yard we fell back from the bridge, firing as furiously as we could at the German masses, and for half a mile we kept up an unequal rearguard struggle. It seemed that we should be hopelessly outnumbered and that there was little hope; then we saw two divisions of the French advancing, and knew that we should pull through. The French came on and gave us help, and, covering our retirement, enabled us to get away from the bridge.

It was in one of the charges on a bridge which was held by the Germans, just before we got to the Aisne, that Prince Maurice distinguished himself. He was very daring and was always one of the first in the fighting, no matter where or what it was. I was not actually in the charge, being in the supports behind; but I saw the charge made, and a grand sight it was to watch our fellows rush forward with the steel and take the bridge. At another time the Prince was in action with a German rearguard and narrowly escaped death. I was in this affair, and saw a German shell burst about a yard away. It plugged into the ground and made a fine commotion and scattered earth and fragments around us; but a chum and myself laughed as we dodged it, and that was the way we got into of taking these explosions when we became used to the war. You could not help laughing, even if you were a bit nervous. During this fight Prince Maurice was shot through the cap, so that he had a shave for his life, but he made light of his escape, and was very proud of the hole in the cap, which he showed to us when he talked with us, as he often did, before he fell.

There were so many incidents of coolness and disregard of wounds that it is not easy to recollect them all; but I call to mind that our adjutant, Lieutenant Woods, was shot in a little affair with the Germans. A sergeant had taken a maxim gun to put in position at a certain spot; but he had gone the wrong way and the adjutant went after him to put things right. He was too late, however, for the sergeant was spotted by the Germans and was killed. The adjutant himself was struck, but managed to get away, and he came back laughing and saying, "Oh! damn those Germans! They've shot me in the leg!" But in spite of the wound he would not lie up or let anybody do anything for him--he bound up the wound himself and carried on. I saw another case, later, which illustrates the coolness of the British officer and his determination not to leave the fight till he is forced to do so. I was by that time wounded and in a temporary hospital, and the artillery were keeping up one of the endless duels. The officer had been struck, and he came into the hospital, and I saw that his hand had been partially blown off; but instead of caving in, as he might well have done, he had the hand bound up and put it in a sling, then he went back to his battery just outside the windows and kept on pounding away at the Germans.

We had plenty of excitement with the German aeroplanes, and often potted at them, but I did not see any of the machines brought down. I remember one day when an aeroplane was trying to locate our position--we were retiring through a French village--and a brigade started firing at it. Just when the aeroplane appeared, the little boys and girls of the village were giving us delicious plums, which they were getting from the trees. We were thoroughly enjoying ourselves, and the youngsters liked it too, when the aeroplane swooped along and we instantly started firing at it. So many rifles going made a tremendous rattle, and the poor little boys and girls were terrified and ran off screaming, and scattered in all directions. We shouted to them and tried to bring them back, but they didn't come, and disappeared in all sorts of hiding-places. The aeroplane got away, I believe, but at any rate it did no mischief at that particular spot. The French civilian folk got used to running off and hiding. In another village we passed through we came to a large house and found that three young ladies and their parents had been forced into the cellar and locked there by the Germans. When we entered the house, the prisoners were starving, and were thankful for anything that we gave them; but they would not take any money from us. The young ladies spoke English quite nicely.

We got quite used to aeroplanes--our own, the Germans, and the French, and saw several thrilling fights in the air. Once we saw a French aeroplane furiously fired on by the Germans--a regular cannonade it was; but the shells and bullets never got at it, and the aeroplane escaped. It was wonderful to see the way the machine shot down, as if nothing could prevent it from smashing on the ground, then to watch it suddenly turn upward and soar away as safely and swiftly as a bird. The airman's idea seemed to be to dodge the fire, and he darted about in such a bewildering fashion that no gunner or rifleman could hope to do anything with him. We were all greatly excited by this thrilling performance in the air, and glad when we knew that the plucky Frenchman had been swift enough to dodge the shells and bullets.

We had had some very trying work to do, and now we were going to get our reward for it. Some of the hardest of the work was that about which people hear nothing, and perhaps never even think--on sentry at night, for instance, about the most nerve-racking job you can imagine. We were always double sentry, and stood for two hours about five yards from each other, like statues, never moving. I always felt funky at this sort of work at the start--you can imagine such a lot in the dark and the strain is so heavy. At the slightest sound the rifle would be presented, and the word "Halt!" ring out--just that word and nothing more, and if there wasn't an instant satisfactory reply it was a bad look-out for the other party. The Germans were very cunning at getting up to some of the British outposts and sentries, and as so many of them speak English very well, they were dangerous customers to tackle, and this added to the heavy strain of sentry work at night.

Now I come to the Battle of the Aisne. I had three days and nights of it before I was bowled out.

A strange thing happened on the first day of the battle, and that was the appearance of a little black dog. I don't know where he came from, or why he joined us, but he followed the battalion all the rest of the time I was with it, and not only that, but he went into action, so he became quite one of us.

Once, in the darkness, we walked into a German outpost. We found it pretty hard going just about there, for the German dead were so thick that we had to walk over them. That march in the night was a wonderful and solemn thing. Three columns of us were going in different directions, yet moving so quietly that you could scarcely hear a sound. All around us, in that Valley of the Aisne, were burning buildings and haystacks, making a terrible illumination, and showing too well what war means when it is carried on by a nation like the Germans, for this burning and destroying was their doing.

Silently, without any talking, we went on, and then we fell into the outpost. I heard the stillness of the night broken by the sharp sound of voices, a sound which was instantly followed by shots, and the furious barking of our little dog, which up to that point had been perfectly quiet. The shots were fired by Captain Woollen, who killed two of the Germans, and one of our men shot a third. We left them where they fell and retired as quickly as we could; but we had done what we started out to do, and that was to find the position of the enemy.

While advancing again we caught a column of Germans. Our brigade-major saw them and came tearing back and told us that they were about fourteen hundred yards to the left of us. Within ten minutes we had a firing line made and our artillery was in position as well. It was a grand sight to see our fellows running into the firing line smoking cigarettes, as cool as if they were doing a bit of skirmishing on training.

We gave the Germans about three hours' hot firing, then a company went round to take the prisoners. The white flag had been shown, but we had not been allowed to take any notice of that until we were sure of our men, because the Germans had so often made a wrong use of the signal of surrender. When the company got round to the Germans it was found that they had already thrown down their rifles. Our brigade took about 500 prisoners, and the rest we handed over to the 1st Division. The Germans had about a mile and a half of convoy, which got away; but the French captured it in the evening, and so made a very nice little complete victory of the affair.

At that time, early in the war, the Germans thought they were going to have it all their own way, and they considered that any trick, white flag or otherwise, was good enough. So certain were they about victory that in one village we passed through we saw written on a wall, in English, evidently by a German, "We will do the tango in Paris on the 13th." We laughed a good deal when we read that boast, and well we might, for it was on the 13th that we saw the writing on the wall, and the Germans by that time were getting driven a long way back from the French capital.

On the Monday morning we went out as flank guard on the Aisne, and were going along behind some hills when our captain spotted swarms of Germans coming up over a ridge about twelve hundred yards away. He ordered two platoons to go out and line the ridge, and for the ridge we went. When we reached it, our captain told us that not a man was to show his head over the ridge until he gave the word to fire.

The Germans came on, getting nearer and nearer, in dense masses, and it was the hardest thing in the world not to let fly at them. They advanced till they were about seven hundred yards away, then we showed them what British rifles could do. We simply went for them, and our rifles got so hot that we could scarcely hold them. Despite that awful hail of bullets the Germans came on, and hurled themselves against us till they were not more than a hundred yards away; then we wanted to charge them, and begged to be let loose with the bayonet, but our captain told us that there were not enough of us to do it. So we retired to our own battalion, the whole of which had the joy of going for them. But the Germans didn't wait for us. They don't like the British steel, and when we had pushed them right back, without actually getting at them, they cleared off.

This was the kind of thing that went on in the Valley of the Aisne. It was work in the open and work in the trenches, on top of the incessant fighting we had had. On the third day, at night, we had just come out of the trenches, having been relieved by another company. We were in good spirits, for we had been sent to a barn, where we were to spend the night. That was a splendid bit of luck, because it meant that we were to get a nice rest and have a good time. The barn had hay in it, and we simply packed the place. It was on a farm, and during the day we had seen the farmer and his wife. There was a village near, with a church and houses, and it had proved a fine target for the Germans, who constantly shelled the place. We had got quite into the way of watching the shells burst about fifty yards in front of us, and it really was a grand sight to sit and gaze at them. We sometimes did this when we were so heavily bombarded that we could do nothing with the rifle or bayonet. Little did we know what was in store for us at the barn from shells.

2

FAREWELL, WHISKERS!

Bert Hall

An American serving in the French Foreign Legion

"Bert Hall, who wrote the article printed herewith, is an American, and has had experience both as a racing automobile driver and an airman. At the beginning of the war he joined the French Foreign Legion, but was afterward transferred to the French Aviation Corps."

*O*ur company had an eight days' "shift" in the trenches, followed by three days' rest at a camp four miles in the rear.

During the week's duty it was impossible to wash or take off one's clothes, and we quickly got into a horrible condition of filth. To begin with, there was a cake of mud from head to foot about half an inch thick; but what was worse was the vermin which infested our clothes almost immediately and were practically impossible to get rid of. They nearly broke the heart of Lieutenant Bloch. He had a wonderful crop of bright red whiskers, of which he was as proud as a kitten with its first mouse, because he thought they gave him a really warlike appearance, and he was always combing them and squinting at them in a little pocket mirror. Well, one day the lice got into these whiskers and fairly gave him hades. He bore it for a week, scratching away at his chin until he was tearing out chunks of hair by the roots; but at last he could stand no more, and had to have the whole lot shaved off. He was the saddest thing you ever saw after that, with a little chinless face like a pink rabbit, and was so ashamed he hardly dared show himself in daylight.

But mud and vermin were only minor worries, really; our proper serious troubles were cold and hunger. It's pretty cool in the middle of France toward the end of November, and for some reason--I guess because they were such a lot of infernal thieves at our depot--we never got any of the clothes and warm wraps sent up from Paris for us. It was just throwing money away to try it. My wife mailed me three or four lots of woollen sweaters and underclothes, but I never received a single thing, and the rest of the boys had much the same experience.

Running the Gauntlet:

That was bad, but the hunger was something fierce. The Foreign Legion is not particularly well fed at any time--coffee and dry bread for breakfast, soup with lumps of meat in it for luncheon, with rice to follow, and the same plus coffee for dinner, and not too much of anything, either. But in our case all the grub had to be brought in buckets from the relief post, four miles away, by squads leaving the trenches at three A. M., ten A. M., and five P. M., and a tough job it was, what with the darkness and the mud and the shell holes and the

German cannonade, to say nothing of occasional snipers taking pot shots at you with rifles. I got one bullet once right between my legs, which drilled a hole in the next bucket in line and wasted all our coffee.

As you can imagine, quite a lot of the stuff used to get spilt on the way, and then the boys carrying it used to scrape it up off the ground and put it back again, so that nearly everything one ate was full of gravel and, of course, absolutely cold. More than once when the cannonade was especially violent we got nothing to eat all day but a couple of little old sardines; and, believe me, it takes a mighty strong stomach to stand that sort of treatment for any length of time. As far as we Americans were concerned, who were mostly accustomed to man-sized meals, the net result was literally slow starvation.

Repulsed With Loss:

The second night in the trenches we had an alarm of a night attack. I crept out to a "funk-hole" some thirty yards ahead of our trench with a couple of friends. It was nearly ten o'clock and there was a thin drizzle. We stared out into the darkness, breathing hard in our excitement. The usual fireworks display of searchlights and rockets over the German trenches was missing--an invariable sign of a contemplated attack, we had been told. Suddenly I glimpsed a line of dim figures advancing slowly through the darkness. "Hold your fire, boys," I gasped. "Let them get good and close before you loose off." They came nearer, stealthily, silently. We raised our rifles. Suddenly my friend on the right rolled over, shaking with noiseless laughter. For a moment we thought he was mad. Then we, too, realised the truth. The approaching column, instead of eager, bloodthirsty Germans, was a dozen harmless domestic cows, strays, doubtless, from a deserted farm. There were considerable casualties among the attacking force, and for a week at least the American section of the Foreign Legion had an ample diet.

The next night the three of us were out there again, but there was still no attack, though we had rather a nasty experience all the same. We were crawling back to our trench about midnight when suddenly we found ourselves under a heavy fire. One bullet went through Thaw's kepi, but we soon saw that instead of coming from the Germans, the fire was directed from a section of our own trenches who thought there was an attack. We yelled, but they went on shooting. I was so mad that I shot back at them, but luckily there was no damage done anywhere.

Praise for Germans:

Two nights later there really did come an attack in considerable force. A lot of us crawled out into a hollow in front of our trench and, starting at about forty yards' distance, we let them have it hot and heavy. We had our bayonets fixed, but they didn't get near enough to charge. I think we kept up America's reputation for marksmanship; anyway, they melted away after about half an hour, and in the morning there were several hundred dead bodies in front of the trench--they had taken the wounded back with them. The bodies were still there when I left, nearly three months later. I crawled out a night or two afterward and had a look at them, and was lucky enough to get an iron cross as a souvenir off a young officer. He was lying flat on his back with a hole between the eyes, and he had the horriblest grin human face ever wore; his lips were drawn right back off the teeth so that he seemed to be snarling like a wild beast ready to bite. We took no prisoners at all; in fact, none of them got near enough, and our Colonel didn't think it worth while risking a counter-charge.

To tell the truth, we hardly took any prisoners any time, except here and there an occasional straggler. I've heard stories about the Dutchies surrendering easily, but you can take it from me that's all bunk. I used to think that one Irishman could lick seventeen Dutchmen; but, believe me, when they get that old uniform on they are a very different proposition. On one occasion a company of the Legion surrounded a Lieutenant and eleven men. They called on them to surrender, but not a bit of it. They held out all day and fought to the last gasp. At last only the Lieutenant and one soldier were left alive, both wounded. Again they refused to give in, and they had to kill the Lieutenant before the last survivor finally threw down his rifle and let them carry him off. I heard he died on the way to the station, and I'm mighty sorry; he was a white man, if he was a German. One remarkable thing about the prisoners we did get was their exceedingly thorough knowledge of everything going on, not only of the war in general, but of all that was taking place back of our trenches. Their spy system is something marvellous. Why, they knew the exact date our reinforcements were coming on one occasion nearly a week beforehand, when the majority of our fellows hadn't even an idea there were any expected! In some cases they got information from French villagers whom they had bought before they retreated. I saw one such case myself. We were bivouacked in a ruined village, and a lot of us were sleeping in and around a cottage that hadn't been damaged. We were downstairs, while the owner of the cottage and his wife and kid had the upstairs room. One of our boys happened to go outside in the night and, by jingo! he saw the fellow coolly signalling with a lamp behind his curtain. He went along and told the Captain, who was at the schoolhouse, and they came back with a couple of under officers and arrested them red-handed. He tried to hide under the bed, and howled for mercy when they pulled him out. His wife never turned a hair--the Sergeant told me she looked as if she was glad he'd been caught. They shot him there and then in his own yard, and his wife was around in the morning just as if nothing had happened.

3

PRIVATE MCGLADE

Writing to his aged mother in County Monaghan, bears witness to the oft-made assertion that the German soldiers object to a bayonet charge:

I am out of it with a whole skin, though we were all beat up, as you might expect after four days of the hardest soldiering you ever dreamed of.

We had our share of the fighting, and I am glad to say we accounted for our share of the German trash, who are a poor lot when it comes to a good, square ruction in the open. We tried hard to get at them many times, but they never would wait for us when they saw the bright bits of steel at the business end of our rifles. Some of our finest lads are now sleeping their last sleep in Belgium, but, mother dear, you can take your son's word for it that for every son of Ireland who will never come back there are at least three Germans who will never be heard of again.

Before leaving Belgium we arranged with a priest to have masses said for the souls of our dead chums, and we scraped together what odd money we had, but his Reverence wouldn't hear of it, taking our money for prayers for the relief of the brave lads who had died so far from the old land to rid Belgian soil of the unmannerly German scrubs.

Some of the Germans don't understand why Irishmen should fight so hard for England, but that just shows how little they know about us.

Seven British soldiers who after the fighting round Mons last week became detached from their regiments and got safely through the German lines arrived in Folkestone to-day from Boulogne. They belonged to the Irish Rifles, Royal Scots, Somerset Light Infantry, Middlesex and Enniskillen Fusiliers, and presented a bedraggled appearance, wearing old garments given them by the French to aid their disguise.

One of the seven, a Londoner, described the fight his regiment had with the Germans at a village near Maubeuge. The British forces were greatly outnumbered by the Germans, but held their ground for twenty-four hours, inflicting very heavy loss on the enemy, although suffering severely itself. He declared that the Germans held women up in front of them when attacking. "It was worse than savage warfare." Paddy, an Irishman, stated that the soldiers got little or no food during the fighting. "When we got our bacon cooking the Germans attacked us." A Scotsman of the party said he saw a hospital flying the Red Cross near Mons destroyed by shrapnel. "When we were ordered to retire," he continued, "we did so very reluctantly. But we did not swear. Things are so serious there, it makes you feel religious.

4

THE STRUGGLE ON THE AISNE

9318 Private HERBERT PAGE 1st Bn. Coldstream Guards

*T*here was fierce fighting all day on Sunday, September 13th, when the Battle of the Aisne began; but the Coldstreamers were not in it till the Monday. We had had a lot of heavy fighting, though, since the beginning of the business at Mons, and we had had a fine fight at Landrecies--a fight which has been specially mentioned in despatches. At the end of it all the men in my company--Number 2-- had their names taken, but I don't know why. Anyway, it was a grand affair, and no doubt some day the real full story of it will be told and everybody will know what the Coldstreamers did there. Landrecies is particularly an affair of the 3rd Coldstreamers.

We had had a very hard time, fighting and marching and sleeping in the open during the cold nights and in thick mud or in trenches that were deep in water; but with it all we kept very cheerful, especially when we knew that we had brought the Germans up with a jerk and were beginning to roll them back.

The Coldstreamers were in the open all day on the Sunday, right on the side of the artillery, behind a big hill, and were very comfortable. The artillery on both sides were hard at it, but the Germans could not get our range and no shells came near us. It was harvest time, and we were lying down on sheaves of wheat, and making ourselves as cosy as we could. That was not altogether easy to do, because it was raining during the best part of the day and everything was rather depressing and very wet. But we put our oil sheets on the ground, our greatcoats over the oil sheets, and straw on the top of ourselves, so that we were really pretty snug, taken altogether. The straw, I fancy, was put there not so much to give us comfort as to hide us from the view of the chaps who were always flying about in the German aeroplanes, trying to spot us and make our positions known to their own gunners.

Our own aeroplanes and the Germans' were very busy during that Sunday, and shells were flying about them on both sides, but I don't think they were doing much mischief. We ourselves were doing very nicely indeed. Our transport came up and issued new biscuits, and we got a pot of jam each--and delicious they were, too. We enjoyed them immensely, and didn't care a rap about the German shells. Our transport was splendid, and we always had something to go on with. There was no fixed time for any meal, there couldn't be, for we used to march about fifty minutes and take ten minutes' halt. If we were on a long day's march we would get an hour or two at dinner-time, usually from one o'clock. It was a funny country we were in, hot in the daytime and cold at night; but we soon got used to that. We were helped enormously by the kindness of the French, and we got on very well with the people and had not much difficulty in making ourselves understood, especially as we picked up a few words of the language--and we could always make signs. When we wanted a drink we would hold out our water-bottles and say "loo," and they laughed and rushed off and filled our bottles with water.

On the way to the Valley of the Aisne we passed through towns and villages where the Germans had been and we saw what outrages they had committed on both people and property. They had recklessly destroyed everything. They had thrown poor people's property out of the windows into the streets and pulled their bedding into the roads to lie on themselves. The Germans acted like barbarians wherever they went--I saw one poor child who was riddled with bullets. We ourselves had strict orders against looting of any sort, but we did not dream of touching other people's property. Whenever we came to a town or village we warned the people to get away, as the Germans were coming, and they went. It was always pleasant to hear them say--as they did to our officers, who spoke to them in French--that they felt safe when the English were there.

The river Aisne runs through lovely country, which looks a bit of a wreck now, because we had to rush across the open and trample down the wheat to get at the Germans. The country's crops were spoiled, but the damage we did was trifling compared with the devastation that the Germans caused.

Throughout that Sunday when the Battle of the Aisne opened we had no casualties, and the day passed pretty well. At night we slept in a barn, which was better than the wet fields. There were no rats, but plenty of rabbits, for the people of the farm seemed to breed them and to have left the hutches open. That night in the barn gave me the best rest I had had since Mons, as I was not even on guard. We had a good breakfast in the barn, tea, bully beef and biscuits, and marched off soon after six in the morning, which was very wet and cold. We marched about four miles, until we came to the Aisne, to a bridge that had been blown up and so shattered that there was only a broken girder left. The rest of the bridge was in the river, which was very deep in the middle, after the heavy rains.

We were now properly in the thick of the battle and a fierce business it was, because the Germans had the range of us and were dropping shells as fast as they could fire. Some of the Guards were got across by boats, but we had to wait our turn to cross over a pontoon bridge which the Engineers had put up, in spite of the heavy fire.

We felt the German artillery fire at this place, near the village of Vendresse, but we could not see them. We watched the Loyal North Lancashires cross the pontoon bridge and saw them march away on the other side of the river, which was well wooded, then we heard them firing hard and knew that they were in action with the Germans. We were not long in following the North Lancashires and over the pontoon bridge we went, going very quietly, as we had been told to make as little noise as possible. In about an hour we were properly in the business ourselves.

After crossing the river we began to feel that at last we were really at the Germans. We made the best of the shelter that the wood gave us, and from behind trees and from the sodden ground we kept up a destructive fire on the enemy, getting nearer to him all the time. Things were growing very hot and the whole countryside rang with the crashing of the guns and the everlasting rattle of the rifles and machine-guns. We were expecting more of our men to cross the river and rein-force us, but the German guns had got the range of the pontoons and no more of our men could cross, so that for the time being we were cut off and had to do as best we could with one of the very strong rearguards of the enemy.

When we had put some good firing in from the wood we left the shelter of the trees and got into the open country, and then we were met by a shell fire which did a great deal of mischief amongst us. These shells were the big chaps that we called Jack Johnsons, and one came and struck an officer of the North Lancashires who was standing on the right of his line. I was not far from him, being on the left of our own line. The shell shattered both his legs and he fell to the ground. I hurried up, and the first thing the officer asked for was a smoke. We propped him up against a haycock and a chap who had some French tobacco made a fag and gave it to the officer--nobody had a cigarette ready made. He smoked half of it and died. By that time the stretcher-bearers had come up and were taking him away. Before he left for the rear I gently pulled his cap over his face. This affair filled the men around with grief, but it put more heart into us to go on fighting the Germans.

Our artillery now began to fire rapidly and the Germans started to retire. There was a big bunch of them, and they made for the hill as fast as they could go, meaning to scuttle down the other side and get away. But our gunners were too sharp for them, and they were properly roused up by that time. They came up in splendid style--the 117th Field Battery, I think they were--and just as the Germans reached the top of the hill in a solid body our gunners dropped three shells straight into them, and three parts of the flying Germans stopped on the top of the hill--dead.

I could not say how many Germans there were against us at this place, but I know that they came on in swarms, and they went down as fast as we could fire. But their going down seemed to make no difference to their numbers. They were only a few hundred yards away, and we could see them quite plainly. They were running all over the place, like a lot of mad sheep, they were so excited. And they were blowing trumpets, like our cavalry trumpets, and beating drums and shouting "Hoch! Hoch!" as hard as they could shout.

They kept blowing their charge and banging their drums till they were about 300 yards away, and shouting their "Hochs!" They shouted other words as well, but I don't know what they were.

When our chaps heard the trumpets and drums going and the German cheers they answered with a good old British "Hooray!" and a lot of them laughed and shouted, "Here comes the Kaiser's rag-time band! We'll give you 'Hoch!' when you get a bit nearer!" And I think we did. At any rate we kept on firing at them all the time they were advancing; but they swept ahead in such big numbers that we were forced to retire into the wood.

As soon as we got into the wood we came under very heavy machine-gun fire from the Germans, and the bullets rained about us, driving into the earth and into the trees and whizzing all around us everywhere. The German shells were smashing after us, too, but were not doing much damage at that point.

It was now that I lost a very old chum of mine, a fine chap from Newcastle named Layden, a private. He was in the thick of the machine-gun fire, a few paces from me, when he suddenly cried out and I knew that he was hit. The first thing he said was, "Give me a cigarette. I know I shan't go on much longer." When we asked him what the matter was he said he was hurt. "Are you wounded?" he was asked. "Yes, I'm hit in the stomach," he answered--and he was, by about seventeen bullets.

The call went round for a cigarette, but nobody had one--lots of cigarettes were sent out to the soldiers that never reached them--but poor Layden was soon beyond the need of fags. He was delirious when our stretcher-bearers came and took him to a barn which had been turned into a temporary hospital. He lingered there for some time; but the last I saw of him was on the field. I missed him badly, because we had been good chums, and whatever we got we used to give each other half of it.

For about five hours, until two o'clock in the afternoon, that part of the battle went on, and all the time we were holding the Germans back; then we were reinforced by the remainder of our troops, who came across the pontoon bridge to our assistance.

The Germans now seemed to think that they had had enough of it and they held up white flags, and we left the shelter of the wood and went out to capture them. I should think that there were about three hundred of the Germans at that point who pretended to surrender by holding up the white flag; but as soon as we were up with them their people behind fired at us--a treacherous trick they practised very often. In spite of it all we managed to get the best part of the prisoners safe and drove them in before us to our own lines. When they really surrendered, and did not play the white flag game, we used to go up and take all their rifles, bayonets and ammunition, and throw them away out of their reach, so that they could not make a sudden dash for them and turn on us. When we had chased a few prisoners and had seen what the Germans meant by the white flag signal, we were told to take no notice of it, but to keep on shooting till they put their hands up.

A lot of the prisoners spoke English and said how glad they were to be captured and have no more fighting to do. Some said they loved England too much to want to fight against us, and a German said, "Long live King George, and blow the Kaiser!" But I don't know how many of them meant what they said--you can't depend on Germans.

We had plenty of talks with the German prisoners who could speak English. Some of them who had lived in England spoke our language quite well, and it was very interesting to hear what they had to say about us and the French and the Belgians. They couldn't stand the British cavalry, and one man said, "We don't like those Englishmen on the grey horses at all," meaning the Scots Greys. Several of the prisoners said they didn't mind so much fighting the French, because the French infantry fired too high, nor the Russians, because they fired too low; "but," they said, "every time the Englishman pulls the trigger he means death." That was a very nice compliment to us, and there was a great deal of truth in what was said about the British rifle fire.

I can assure you that when we settled down to the work we often enough plugged into the Germans just as if we were on manoeuvres.

At the very first--and I'm not ashamed to say it--I shook like a leaf and fired anyhow and pretty well anywhere; but when that first awful nervousness had passed--not to return--we went at it ding-dong all the time and fired as steadily as if we were on the ranges. The men were amazingly cool at the business--and as for the officers, well, they didn't seem to care a rap for bullets or shells or anything else, and walked about and gave orders as if there were no such things in the world as German soldiers.

Most of the poor beggars we took were ravenous for want of food, and those who could speak English said they had been practically without food for days, and we saw that they had had to make shift with the oats that the horses were fed with. This starvation arose from the fact that a few days earlier we had captured the German transport and left them pretty short of food.

That rush after the Germans and bagging them was exciting work. It was successful and everything seemed to be going very well. But there was a nasty surprise in store for me and one which very nearly ended my career as a fighting man. I had really a miraculous escape.

I had charge of about four prisoners, and kept them well in front of me, so that they could not rush me. I kept them covered with my rifle all the time, and as I had ten rounds in my magazine I knew that they wouldn't have a ghost of a chance if they tried any German tricks on me--I could easily have finished the lot before they could have got at me.

As I was driving the prisoners I felt as if some one had come up and punched me on the ear. I did not know whether I had been actually hit by somebody or shot, but I turned my head and at once fell to the ground. I was swiftly up again on my feet and scrambled about. I knew that I was hurt, but the thing I mostly cared about just then was my bag of prisoners, so I handed them over to another man, and he took them in. I then found that I had been shot in the neck by a bullet. It had gone in at the collar of the jacket, at the back of the neck-- here's the hole it made--and through the neck and out here, where the scar is, just under the jaw. A narrow shave? Yes, that's what the doctor said--it had just missed the jugular vein. The shot bowled me out, but it was a poor performance by the German who fired, because he could not have been more than three hundred yards away, and being six foot one I made a big target at that short distance. Anyway, he missed me and I was told to go to a barn not far away which had been turned into a hospital, bed mattresses having been placed on the floor. Here my kit was taken off me and I was looked after at once, my kit being given to a North Lancashire man who had lost his own and had been without one for three days. He had been in a small battle and had had to take his choice between dropping his kit and being caught; so he got rid of his kit and was able to escape. When he left the barn he went into the firing line, but he only lasted about ten minutes there. I had seen him leave and I saw him brought back by the stretcher-bearers. As soon as he was inside the barn he asked where I was, and he was told and was laid down close to me. "Look here, old chap," he said pleasantly, "if you'd only been ten minutes later I shouldn't have been here, because I shouldn't have got your kit and gone into the firing line and got hit."

Perhaps he was right. He might have escaped; but as it was he had been shot through both legs.

I didn't like being in the barn and out of the fighting. It was better to be in the firing line, with all its excitement and the knowledge that you were doing your bit to help things along and drive the Germans back to the best place for them, and that's Germany; but our officers, who never lost a chance of cheering and helping us, came in when they could to see how we were getting on. During the afternoon my company officer, Captain Brocklehurst, and the adjutant, came in to see how things were going. Captain Brocklehurst saw me and said, "There are not many of the company left; but we're doing wonderfully well. We've killed a good many of the Germans and taken about five hundred prisoners." That was good news, very good, but it was even better when the captain added, "And we're pushing them back all the time."

The guns were booming and the rifles were crackling all around us while we were lying in the barn, and wounded men were being constantly brought in, keeping the doctors and the ambulance men terribly busy--and you can imagine what it must have meant for the Germans if it was like that for us; because we fought in open order, so that we were not easy to hit, whereas the Germans were in their solid formation, which meant that they could not advance against the British fire without being mown down.

I was in the barn, which was crowded with wounded, till about one o'clock in the morning, then we were taken in Red Cross vans to another hospital about three miles away, and as we left the French people showed us all the kindness they could, giving us water, milk and food, in fact all they had. We crossed the pontoon bridge and were put into another barn which had been turned into a hospital, and we stayed there for the night. We left that place in the morning for La Fère, about twenty miles away. There were a great many motor waggons being used as ambulances, and they were all needed, because of the crowds of wounded. All of us who could walk had to do so, as all the vans and lorries were wanted for the bad cases. I could manage to walk for about a mile at a stretch, but I could not use my arms. When I had done a mile, I rested, then went on again, and so I got to the end of the journey, with a lot more who were just about able to do the same. We didn't grumble, because we were thankful to be able to walk at all and not to be so badly wounded that we could not shift for ourselves. When we got to La Fère the hospital was so full that we were put straight into a hospital train, and I was in it for two days and nights, stopping at stations for brief halts. Again the French people were kindness itself and pressed food and drink on us. We got to Nantes, where my wound was dressed and we had supper, and then I had what seemed like a taste of heaven, for I was put into a proper bed. Yes, after sleeping for so many nights on the ground, anyhow and anywhere, often enough in mud and water, it was like getting into heaven itself to get into a bed. On the Saturday they put us on board a ship and took us round to Liverpool, a four days' journey on the sea. First we went to Fazackerley, and then I was lucky enough to be sent on to Knowsley Hall, where Lady Derby, who has a son in France with the Grenadiers, had turned the state dining-room into a hospital ward. There were sixteen Guardsmen in the ward, with four trained nurses to look after us. Wasn't that a contrast to the barns and flooded trenches! Now I'm back in London, feeling almost fit again, and soon I shall have to report myself.

I have only told you about the little bit I saw myself of the tremendous Battle of the Aisne. Considering the length of it and the fearful nature of the firing, it sometimes strikes me as a very strange thing that I should be alive at all; but stranger still that some men went through it all, right away from the beginning at Mons, and escaped without a scratch.

5

A SOLDIER WHO BAYONETS HIS FIRST BOCHE

Gustav P Capart– Belgium, September, 1914

A young soldier was seated alongside the road. He belonged to a Regiment of the Division quartered in the neighbouring villages. He had a sad and dejected air.

I seated myself at his side because I wanted to know the impression of the men who had already been in battle.

"Have you been under fire?" I queried. "Yes, corporal."

How many Germans have you killed?" I saw a haze of anger pass over the eyes of this young chap who regarded me with a fixed look.

Just one! I hate the Germans, I swear it, but I tremble to think what I have done--yes, I killed him dead enough!

Voilà! I am a gardener by trade. I live in the Luxembourg. The garden of my masters--it is all my life. Why has this accursed war broken out? Can they no longer stay at home, the pigs?

Then I was called and you know the rest, because I will not speak of the first days of the campaign.

"But, _voilà!_ one night we made an ambuscade on a farm in the outskirts of Vilvorde. It was dark. They told us the Germans would possibly attempt a reconnaissance in the village and it was necessary to open their eyes.

We were placed in a house closer to the enemy lines than the others and it was forbidden to enter the street. Some of my comrades were hidden above on the second floor, but I was hiding back of the front stairs and observed the entrance-way.

My nerves were overexcited by this long wait. A single ray of the moon wandered over the ground above the gate; it recalled one of my ambushes for flower poachers.

Night advanced and finally I believed they would never come. Suddenly a well-sustained fire broke out a short distance away. I had fixed my bayonet and now grasped my rifle tightly.

The gate opened brusquely. The night was clear and I saw a big devil of a German officer, revolver in hand, pass through and enter the walk. He desired without doubt to seek shelter, for he slammed the gate after him.

This is what passed then in a flash. I left my hiding place--he saw me. In his eyes there was the look of distress one always sees in those of a trapped beast. He shot at me, but so quickly that he did not aim. The report awoke the whole house.

Already I had jumped at him--and I literally nailed him to the gate.

Ah! To feel the crushing of bones--when one is accustomed to cultivate flowers--to feel the crushing of bones!

6

THE MOST CRITICAL DAY OF ALL

Corporal Frederick William Holmes, VC, 2nd Battalion The King's
Own (Yorkshire Light Infantry)

FOR SEVEN YEARS I was with the colours in the old 51st, which is now the Yorkshire Light Infantry, then I was drafted to the Reserve; but I was called back only a fortnight later, when the war broke out.

The regimental depot is at Pontefract, in South Yorkshire, which some unkind people say is the last place that God started and never finished, and in August, having become a soldier again, after marrying and settling down to civil life in Dublin, I found myself in a region which was almost like the South Yorkshire coalfields. There were the same pit-heads and shale-heaps, so that you could almost think you were in England again--but how different from England's calmness and security! It was around these pit-heads and shale-heaps that some of the fiercest fighting of the earlier days of the war took place.

We had left Dublin and reached Havre at midnight; we had been to the fortified town of Landrecies, where the Coldstreamers were to do such glorious things, and had got to Maroilles, where Sir Douglas Haig and the 1st Division became heavily engaged. We were at Maroilles, in billets, from the 18th to the 21st. Billets meant almost anything, and we lived and slept in all sorts of places as well as the trenches--but being in the open in summer was no hardship. The fields had been harvested and we often slept on the stacks of corn.

The people were really most kind; they gave us every mortal thing as we marched, beer, wine, cigarettes and anything else there was.

At five o'clock on the Saturday afternoon we were billeted in a brewery, where we stayed till Sunday noon, when, as we were having dinner, shells were bursting and beginning things for us. We were ordered to take up a position about two miles from Mons, and on that famous Sunday we went into action near a railway embankment.

People by this time know all about Mons, so I will only say that after that hard business we retired towards Le Cateau, after fighting all day on the 24th and all the following night. After that we took up a position on outpost and stayed on outpost all night, then, at about two in the morning, we dropped into some trenches that we had previously occupied.

I know what Mons was and I went through the battles of the Marne and the Aisne; but nothing I had seen could be compared for fury and horror with the stand of the 5th Division on the 26th. It was essentially a fight by the 5th, because that was the only division employed at Le Cateau. The division was composed of three brigades, the 12th, 13th and 14th. My battalion, the 2nd Yorkshire Light Infantry, was in the 13th, the other battalions with us being the West Riding, the King's Own Scottish Borderers and the West Kent.

There were some coal-pit hills in front of us and the Germans advanced over them in thousands. That was about eleven o'clock in the morning, and the firing began in real earnest again.

The Germans by this time were full of furious hope and reckless courage, because they believed that they had got us on the run and that it was merely a question of hours before we were wiped out of their way. Their blood was properly up, and so was ours, and I think we were a great deal hotter than they were, though we were heavily outnumbered. We hadn't the same opinion of German soldiers that the Germans had, and as they rushed on towards us we opened a fire from the trenches that simply destroyed them.

Some brave deeds were done and some awful sights were seen on the top of the coal-pits. A company of Germans were on one of the tops and an officer and about a dozen men of the "Koylis" went round one side of the pit and tried to get at them. Just as they reached the back of the pit the German artillery opened fire on the lot, Germans and all-- that was one of their tricks. They would rather sacrifice some of their own men themselves than let any of ours escape--and they lost many in settling their account with the handful of Englishmen who had rushed behind the pit at a whole company of Germans.

Hereabouts, at the pits, the machine-gun fire on both sides was particularly deadly. Lieutenant Pepys, who was in charge of the machine-gun of our section, was killed by shots from German machine-guns, and when we went away we picked him up and carried him with us on the machine-gun limber until we buried him outside a little village in a colliery district.

He was a very nice gentleman and the first officer to go down. When he fell Lieutenant N. B. Dennison, the brigade machine-gun officer, took charge. He volunteered to take over the gun, and was either killed or wounded. Then Lieutenant Unett, the well-known gentleman jockey, crawled on his stomach to the first line of the trenches, with some men, dragging a machine-gun behind them. They got this gun into the very front of the line of the trenches, then opened fire on the Germans with disastrous effect. Lieutenant Unett was wounded and lay in the open all the time.

This gallant deed was done between twelve noon and one o'clock, and I was one of the few men who saw it. I am glad to be able to pay my humble tribute to it. There was a battery of the Royal Field Artillery on our left rear, about 800 yards behind the front line of trenches. Our gunners had such excellent range on the Germans that the German gunners were finding them with high explosive shell. It was mostly those shells that were dropping on them till they got the range and killed the gunners. There were only about five who were not either killed or wounded. The officer was wounded; but in spite of that he carried a wounded man round the bottom of the hill, then went back and fetched another man and repeated the journey until he had taken every one of the five away. After that he returned, picked up a spade and smashed the sights of the gun and made it useless. We heard some time afterwards that he had been killed.

This brave deed was witnessed by most of us who were in the front line of trenches.

When the German guns were got into position in front of us and the Germans tried their hardest to blow us out of our trenches, they searched for our artillery and, failing to discover it, they grew more determined than ever to rout us out of the place from which we were doing deadly damage.

In spite of the heavy losses around us we held on, and all the more stubbornly because we expected every moment that the French would come up and reinforce us. The French were due about four o'clock, but owing to some accident they did not arrive, and it seemed as if nothing could save us.

There was a falling off in our artillery fire, and it was clear that one of our batteries had been put out of action. And no wonder, for the German guns were simply raining shells upon us. The Germans at that time were sticking to the dense formations which had been their practice since the war began--and they hurled themselves forward in clouds towards the 37th Field Battery.

So furiously did they rush, so vast were their numbers, and so certain were they that they had the guns as good as captured, that they actually got within a hundred yards of the battery.

It was at this terrible crisis that Captain Douglas Reynolds and volunteers rushed up with two teams and limbered up two guns, and in spite of all the German batteries and rifles did one gun was saved. This was a wonderful escape, in view of the nearness of the German infantry and their numbers, and for their share in the desperate affair the captain and two of the drivers--Drane and Luke--who had volunteered, got the Victoria Cross.

In a way we had got used to retiring, and we were not at the end of it even now, by a good deal, for on our left the Borderers were withdrawing and on our right the Manchesters were being forced right back; fighting magnificently and leaving the ground littered with their dead and wounded.

The Yorkshire Light Infantry were left in the centre of the very front line of the trenches, where we were heavily pressed. We made every mortal effort to hold our ground, and C Company was ordered up from the second line to reinforce us in the first.

Imagine what it meant for a company of infantry to get from one trench to another at a time like that, to leave shelter, to rush across a space of open ground that was literally riddled with shrapnel and rifle bullets, and in the daytime, too, with the Germans in overwhelming force at point-blank range.

But the order had been given, and C Company obeyed. The men sprang from their trench, they rushed across a fire-swept zone--and the handful of them who were not shot down made a final dash and simply tumbled into our trench and strengthened us. They had just about lost their first wind, but were soon hard at it again with the rifle and did murderous work, if only to get something back on account of the comrades who had fallen.

It was a help, a big help, to have C Company with us in the front trench; but even with this reinforcement we could do nothing, and after we had made a hot stand the order came to retire. That was about half-past four in the afternoon.

Things had been bad before; they were almost hopeless now, for to retire meant to show ourselves in the open and become targets for the German infantry; but our sole chance of salvation was to hurry away--there was no thought of surrender. When the order was given there was only one thing to do--jump out of the trenches and make a rush, and we did both; but as soon as we were seen a storm of bullets struck down most of the men.

At such a time it is every man for himself, and it is hardly possible to think of anything except your own skin. All I wanted to do was to obey orders and get out of the trench and away from it.

I had rushed about half-a-dozen yards when I felt a curious tug at my boot. I looked to see what was the matter and found that my foot had been clutched by a poor chap who was wounded and was lying on the ground unable to move.

"For God's sake, save me!" he cried, and before I knew what was happening I had got hold of him and slung him across my back. I can't pretend to tell you details of how it was all done, because I don't clearly remember. There was no time to think of much besides the bullets and the fastest way of getting out of their reach. Rain was falling, not heavily, but it was drizzling, and this made the ground greasy and pretty hard going.

I had not gone far before the poor chap complained that my equipment hurt him and begged me to get it out of his way. The only thing to be done was to drop the equipment altogether, so I halted and somehow got the pack and the rest of it off, and I let my rifle go, too, for the weight of the lot, with the weight of a man, was more than I could tackle.

I picked my man up again, and had struggled on for twenty or thirty yards when I had to stop for a rest.

Just then I saw the major of the company, who said, "What's the matter with him?"

I could not speak, so I pointed to the man's knees, which were shot with shrapnel; then the major answered, "All right! Take him as far as you can, and I hope you'll get him safely out of it."

I picked him up again and off I went, making straight over the hill at the back of the position we had taken, so that he should be safe from the German fire. The point I wanted to reach was about a mile away, and it was a dreadful journey; but I managed to do it, and when I had got there, after many rests, I started to carry my man to the nearest village, which was some distance off.

I got to the village, but the German heavy shells were dropping so fast that I could not stay there, and they told me to carry him into the next village. I was pretty well worn out by this time, but I started again, and at last with a thankful heart I reached the village and got the man into a house where wounded men were being put.

How far did I carry him?

Well, it was calculated that the distance was three miles; but I never felt the weight. Yes, he was quite conscious and kept on moaning and saying, "Oh!" and telling me that if ever he got out of it he would remember me; but I said that he mustn't talk such nonsense--for I wanted him to stop thanking me and to keep his spirits up.

I don't know how long I was in getting him over the ground, for I had no idea of time.

Having put my man in safety I left the house and began to go back to the position, expecting to find some of the regiments to rejoin, but when I reached the firing line there were no regiments left. They had been forced to retire, and the ground was covered with the dead and wounded, as it was impossible to bring all the wounded away.

There was a road at this particular point, and on reaching the top of it I saw the Germans advancing, about 500 yards away. Between them and myself there was a field-gun, with the horses hooked in, ready to move off; but I saw that there was only a wounded trumpeter with it.

I rushed up to him and shouted, "What's wrong?"

"I'm hurt," he said. "The gun has to be got away; but there's nobody left to take it."

I looked all around, and saw that there were no English gunners left-

-there were only the Germans swarming up, 500 yards away and badly wanting to get at the gun.

There was not a second to lose. "Come on," I said, and with that I hoisted the trumpeter into the saddle of the near wheel horse, and clambering myself into the saddle of the lead horse we got the gun going and made a dash up the hill.

There was only the one road, and this was so littered up and fenced about with wire entanglements. that we could not hope to escape by it. Our only chance was by dashing at the hill, and this we did—and a terrible business it was, because we were forced to gallop the gun over the dead bodies of our own men—mostly artillerymen, they were. Many of the poor chaps had crawled away from their battery and had died on the hillside or on the road.

We carried on over the hill, and when the Germans saw what we were doing they rained shells and bullets on us. One or two of the horses were hit, and a bullet knocked my cap off and took a piece of skin from my head—just here. But that didn't hurt me much, nor did another bullet which went through my coat. We carried on, and got over the hill, just driving straight ahead, for we couldn't steer, not even to avoid the dead.

I daresay the bullet that carried off my cap stunned me a bit, at any rate I didn't remember very much after that, for the time being; all I know is that we galloped madly along, and dashed through two or three villages. There was no one in the first village; but in the second I saw an old lady sitting outside a house, with two buckets of water, from which soldiers were drinking. She was rocking to and fro, with her head between her hands, a pitiful sight. Shells were dropping all around and the place was a wreck.

I carried on at full stretch for about ten miles, tearing along to get to the rear of the column. I don't remember that I ever looked back; but I took it that the trumpeter was still in the saddle of the wheel horse.

At last I caught up with the column; then I looked round for the trumpeter, but he was not there, and I did not know what had become of him. That was the first I knew of the fact that I had been driving the gun by myself.

Willy-nilly I had become a sort of artilleryman, and from that time until the 28th I attached myself to the guns; but on that day I rejoined what was left of my old regiment.

I had been in charge of twelve men, but when I inquired about them I found that only three were left—nine had been either killed or wounded, and the rest of the battalion had suffered in proportion. That gives some idea of the desperate nature of the fighting and the way in which the little British army suffered during the first three days after Mons.

The officer who had seen me carrying the man off did not see me go back, but a sergeant who knew me noticed me passing through the village with the gun and he was the first man of my battalion that I saw. This was Sergeant Marchant, who, for his gallantry in helping another sergeant, who was wounded, was awarded the Distinguished Conduct Medal. In that fine affair he was helped by Company-Sergeant-Major Bolton, and both of them were mentioned in despatches.

Of course I never thought of saying anything about what I had done; but I was sent for and asked if it was true, and I said I had got the man away and helped to take the gun off, and this was confirmed by the major who had seen me carrying the man.

For the day's work at Le Cateau two Victoria Crosses were given to my regiment—one to Major C. A. L. Yate, "Cal," he was called, because of his initials, and one to myself.

Major Yate was a very fine officer. He joined us and took command of B Company just before we went out to the war. On this day he was in the trenches, on our left rear, not very far from where I was. When we went "in to action he had 220 men, but they caught so much of the hot fire which was meant for the battery behind that he lost all his men except nineteen when he was surrounded and captured. The day before this happened the major declared that if it came to a pinch and they were surrounded he would not surrender—and he did not surrender now. Reckless of the odds against him he headed his nineteen men in a charge against the Germans—and when that charge was over only three of the company could be formed up. All the freshmen of B Company were either killed or wounded or taken prisoners, though very few prisoners were taken. The major was one of them; but he was so badly wounded that he lived only a very short time, and died as a prisoner of war. His is one of the cases in which the Cross is given although the winner of it is dead.

Major Yate was an absolute gentleman and a great favourite with us all. He had a lot of experience in the Far East and at home, and I am sure that if he had lived he would have become a general. He was always in front, and his constant cry was "Follow me!"

From Le Cateau we got to the Valley of the Aisne and were in trenches for ten days. At midnight on September 24th we advanced two miles beyond the river, which we had crossed by pontoons because all the other bridges had been blown up.

We reached a little village and stayed there in shelters underneath the houses, where all the inhabitants slept. We stayed in one of these cellars and went on outpost at four in the morning and came off at four next morning, then went on again at four a.m.

We were only 250 yards from the Germans, who were in a small wood outside the village, opposite the houses. They had snipers out and were sniping at us all the time. We barricaded the windows of the houses and knocked bricks out of the walls to make loopholes, and through these loopholes we sniped the Germans, and they did their level best to pick us off too. Every time your head was shown a dozen bullets came, and you could not see where they came from. Two or three of our men were killed by snipers; but there was no real chance of getting to grips, for there was barbed wire everywhere, and nothing could be done till this was cut. Night was the only time when the wire could be cut—and night work was both eerie and nerve-racking.

We had "listeners" to listen for any movement by the enemy. A sentry in peace times means a man who walks up and down, smartly dressed, but in war time, at night, he is a listener, and in the daytime he is a "watcher"—he can see in the daytime and hear at night. That is one of the little things which show how greatly war changes the customs of peace.

It was outside Béthune, when we were in reserve to the rest of the brigade, that I was wounded. We had got well into October and we were behind trenches, with French infantry on our right. At night we advanced on a level with the firing line, and in the darkness we dug trenches. We were then next to the King's Own Scottish Borderers.

We finished the trenches before the early hours of the morning and stuck in them till five in the afternoon, when we heard some shouts, and on looking over we saw that the Germans were making a charge.

We opened rapid fire and the Germans answered very smartly, having dropped down. But they were not down long, for up they sprang and with further shouts on they came and got within three hundred yards of us. Then we were ordered to fix bayonets and be ready to charge at any moment; but before we started charging we rushed into another line of trenches in front of us, and there we mixed with the Borderers.

This fight in the night was a thrilling affair, the chief guide on each side being the flashes of the rifles, and these were incessant. The Germans were firing rapidly at anything they could see; but there was little to see except the tiny forks of flame. They must have heard us, however, and that, of course, would help them. One strange thing happened when we reached the trench, and that was that we had to wake up some of the men. In spite of the fighting they were sleeping— but war turns everything upside down, and the British soldier reaches a point when it takes a lot to disturb him.

Suddenly, at this crisis, I felt as if my leg had been struck by something that vibrated, like a springboard, and I dropped down. I was dizzy, but did not think I was hit, and I supposed that if I stayed down for a few minutes I should be all right and able to go on. So I sat down, but quickly found that I could not move, and on feeling my leg I discovered that it was wet and warm, and I knew what that meant, so I took off my equipment and put it down and began to crawl back to the trench I had left when we charged.

I crawled across a mangel-wurzel field to a house of some sort, then I must have become unconscious, for the next thing I knew was that I was being carried along on a stretcher.

It was only yesterday that a friend in my battalion wrote to tell me that we were crawling pretty close together through the mangel-wurzel field. He was shot in the arm and stopped two of the Borderers' stretcher-bearers just in time to have me put on a stretcher.

I had a natural walking-stick which I had cut from a vine, and of which I was very fond. I had fastened it to my rifle and was so proud of it that I said I would carry it through the war, if I could. My friend must have known how I prized the vine-stick, for when he was sent home he brought it with him, and it's waiting for me when I leave hospital.

I also had a letter from my company officer a few days ago. He says he missed me that night, but he could not make out what had happened. He heard that a complete set of equipment had been found, and on learning that I was wounded he assumed that it was mine, and that I had been carried away and left it. He told me that on the very night I "they were relieved by the French infantry, and that he himself was hit ten days afterwards. It was the day before I was wounded that I heard that I was recommended for the French Military Medal, and that was as big a surprise to me as the news that I had been given the Victoria Cross.

That equipment of mine had a tragic history. During the first day of the Aisne I was without equipment and set to work to get some. A bugler of my battalion had been killed by shrapnel and I was told by my officer to go and get his equipment. "Treat him gently, poor chap," said the officer, and you may be sure I did. I helped myself, and thinking that the poor lad's mother might like a memento I brought away his "iron-rations" tin. This is riddled with bullet-holes, just as the bugler was.

There is one thing more that I would like to say, and it is about my birthday, which falls on September 7th. As I had left the colours and gone into the Reserve I thought I could look forward to a fine celebration of the anniversary. And there was a fine celebration, too, for on September 7th our retiring before the Germans ended and we started to advance and drive them back.

Could any British soldier want a finer birthday celebration than that?

7

HOLDING ON

Captain David Fallon, MC. First Division of the Australian
Expeditionary Force
(Gallipoli 1915)

*O*ur little fortress or "sangar" could be likened to a cauldron for it was constantly surrounded by fire--the bursting, flaming shells, and the pepper of snipers' bullets like the sharp bubbling of boiling water to "carry on" the likeness of a cauldron. Down on the beach at the first ridge of rocky embankment the engineers had most bravely under a frightful fire blasted great dug-outs for the establishment of headquarters, a hospital, and the first station for the storing of supplies.

There never was an instant's cessation of the storm of Turkish shells from the batteries back of the cliffs, but other little companies like my own had gained a foot-hold on the first ridge and held on desperately.

Something like organisation was coming out of the chaos. My men were showing no signs of panic. I dispatched two messengers back to the beach to report my position, the number of men still with me, and to secure food and ammunition. These men in common with other messengers sent from similar small strongholds on the ridge, had a most dangerous duty to perform. They ran the gamut of intense fire. Many of them were killed. But my men successfully returned. They came laden with bully beef, biscuits and jam.

Our emergency rations had disappeared hours before and we were brisk enough in opening the boxes and tins and strengthening ourselves with bully beef, biscuits and jam.

The organisation at headquarters went on with remarkable efficiency considering the stormy environment. I soon received a reinforcement which brought my reduced company of twelve men up to my original quota of sixty.

In the protection of night relays of messengers worked briskly in bringing to us rifles and ammunition to complete our supplies. Not that these messengers had any easy pathway. The storm of shrapnel was ceaseless and it was a bright night. We were as grateful for the ammunition as for the food because, as I have already told, all the men of my detachment had been blown into the water and in the saving of their own lives had necessarily abandoned their cartridge belts.

The Turks were still firmly holding a ridge some eighty feet above us from which throughout the night they kept up a playful attack of machine guns, and their snipers were tireless. My men were so annoyed at these attentions that I had some difficulty in restraining them from making sorties. One of the men recklessly stuck his head above the rocky wall of the "sangar" and queried:

"Where are the Turks?"

"Over there," I said, with a nod toward the ridge.

"Don't they ever show themselves?" he demanded indignantly.

"Put your head down, get down, you chump, or you'll never live to see one of them," I told him.

Another time a sniper's bullet ricochetted around the rocky wall of the "sangar." "What's that?" demanded one of my men.

"A ricochet," I replied.

"Don't we use them, too?" asked this guileless rookie.

Fortunately for us the Turks on the ridge above were not possessed of bombs. They tried to make up for this deficiency by hurling at us huge chunks of rock that had been smashed by our battle-ship attack from the face of their sandstone cliffs.

We made them a better retort. We took our bully beef tins and jam tins and tobacco tins, loaded them with broken stones and cordite taken from our rifle cartridges, and messengers were dispatched to return with other forms of explosives and fuses to aid us in the completion of these amateur weapons of war. We lighted them from our cigarette ends and hurled them in whatever direction a Turk had betrayed his presence. Sometimes they would explode prematurely and not a few of the bombers of that night had their faces blown away.

Dawn found us still in possession of the first ridge. While we remained there inactive and before any order had been given to indicate that we were to assault the upper ridge, there came an order which aroused my wonder and opposition. It was to "Fix bayonets!"

Obedience to this order all along our position brought about a startling betrayal of the whereabouts of the entire force, for the sunshine glittered brilliantly on the steel blades and fairly telegraphed the location of all our quotas to the enemy above.

I knew there must be some mistake and cried to my men, "Unfix bayonets! Who the hell gave that order?"

I never found out, but I have very definite suspicion. I am certain it was a false order circulated by spies, which we were subsequently to discover were among us.

It is a fact that the German spy system even invaded the very personnel of the British army. My platoon sergeant, Merrifield, summarily accounted for one of these spies. This was some weeks later, at the attack at Lone Pine. We had won the position and we were consolidating, improving upon the trenches and the strongholds which we had captured when the order come down from the left, "Retire! to the first line."

I shouted "Stick where you are! Who gave that damned order?"

I sent up Merrifield to make inquiries and as he was making his way along the line asking the men where the order had come from, it was pointed out to him that a man on the left started the order. Merrifield went up to him and asked who gave that order to retire. This man replied "Lieutenant Wilhelm." We had seen enough of spy work since we left Australia and Merrifield, rushing up, faced Wilhelm. He did not stop to question him. He read in the man's countenance the appearance of a Teuton, the broad face, high cheek-bones and broad neck. And Merrifield took long chances but was too enraged to consider that. "You damned square-head," he shouted, and with the utterance of the words killed the lieutenant with his bayonet. Wilhelm's attempted treachery not only cost him his life, but did not gain its end, for the order never got any farther. On examining his person, we found letters, photographs and a signal code, all going to show that however recklessly he had acted, Merrifield had made no mistake.

The night of the second day found us in positions higher up among the sandy table lands and ridges and dug into positions that we were to hold for a few weeks waiting for reinforcements, which were coming up from Egypt.

The Turkish snipers occupied a great deal of our attention all this time and they were a cunning lot. They were adepts in the art of camouflage--an art which was new to battlefields at this time. Their favourite method of deception was to paint their bodies green, to shroud their heads with the natural foliage of the country, moss and holly-bush twigs. With this arrangement they could conceal themselves as neatly and completely as snakes in the grass. They not only hid in the shrubbery, but successfully concealed themselves in the stunted trees that grew among the rocky crevices. The cliffs themselves gave them a tremendous advantage. In this they had drilled shooting boxes--holes in all manner of secret recesses large enough to hold their bodies.

But we did not permit them to pot us wholly undisturbed. Many of our men made night expeditions that silenced forever our hidden hunters. One of my bush men came back from such an expedition with a startling souvenir. It was nothing less than a head of one of the Turkish snipers--the face of the ghastly object painted green, twigs enmeshed in the hair and sticking out of the ears. But after a while we were to meet the Turk and find him not such a bad fellow. I asked the prisoners we captured why they were fighting. They said, they didn't know what they were fighting for, but they just wanted to have a fight. A rejoinder which an Irishman like myself could appreciate. In a conversation with an educated Turk I asked him why they allowed the Germans to be the master. He replied that the Germans had for the last forty years over-run his country and taken over the direction of the civil, the military and the naval affairs of his nation, and they were so strong, dealt with the Turks with such an iron hand, that there was no commencing a mutiny. It had been tried and proved a fiasco.

During the months of July and August when the sun was very hot and the ground very dry, and the flies and the mosquitoes were everywhere, water became scarce, for it was a waterless land we were on. The Turkish prisoners, so friendly did they become with us, went back to their own lines and brought us water. We sent others back to try and persuade their kind to come over and give themselves up. We fed them well, gave them the best that we had, and made jolly good fellows of them, as they were indeed. They had given us a good fight and we appreciate a good fighter. Though they went back to their own lines they would always return and brought us frequently gourds of fresh water. The water that we got ourselves was coming from Murdos and

Lemnos Islands. It was brackish and it stunk. We were only allowed one pint per man a day, a stingy ration under a tropic sun. The Turks said they brought us water because when wounded Turks lay gasping for water, we had given them of our own.

Then the time came when we were getting an extra supply of jam, and there were only two kinds of jam issued--plum and an apple and apricot combination. Of course, that set us all grumbling, soldier-like, because we didn't get strawberry. One day one of the men hit upon the idea of exchanging this jam with wine with which the French soldiers over Suvla Bay way were liberally supplied. This exchange went on for about a fortnight, and there were happy times in the trenches. Then the French got fed up with this sameness of jam and our stocks dropped below zero. So we had to look out for another customer. One of our boys hit upon the idea of exchanging the jam with the Turks. During the day we put up our articles of exchange--jam and bully beef on bayonets and held them up in prominent positions on the front line trenches. And we waited anxiously as to what was going to happen, and lo! at night we heard and saw the Turks crawling through the brushwood and scrub, growling and muttering to themselves as their whiskers were caught on the twigs of the bushes. When they reached the front-line trenches they took off the articles of exchange and put in their place wines, cigarettes and Turkish "delight," as we always called the tobacco. That showed us that they didn't want war and we knew we didn't want war, but the Germans wanted it and as long as they wanted it we had to keep going.

Likewise we had other experiences that were not all grim, but they were exciting. For instance, our bathing parties on the beach. We didn't have to bother with bathing suits or summer-resort regulations, but we had the novelty of bathing to the accompaniment of shell fire. When we saw shells diving we dived to get out of the way.

Gallipoli at this period of the year was a frying pan. Men found their uniforms intolerable. We cut our trousers into "knickers," abandoned our tunics, and did all our fighting in bare knees and shirt sleeves. Our enemies got a wrong impression from this. Turkish prisoners told us that the report among them was we were falling so short of supplies that we were cutting our trousers in two to make double the number of pairs. The idea of our poverty of supplies was further strengthened by the fact that many of our men abandoned shirts entirely and moved about like savages with bronzed bodies naked of all covering save the knickers and their socks and boots. Our aspect and the fact that our men went after them practically always with a bayonet, won for us from the Turk the respectful sobriquet of the "White Ghurkas," the Ghurkas being famous for their fondness and expertness in the use of the knife.

Not to give the reader too happy an impression of affairs as they stood with us in Gallipoli after the night of our desperate landing, it might be well to note here that of our original landing force of 20,000 there had been at least 5,000 casualties among us. The night of the landing in the storm from the Turkish forts, the cliff batteries, the machine guns and the snipers, and also the drownings, fully 3,000 men had been killed or wounded. In the intermittent fighting of the following weeks preceding the attacks on Lone Pine and Chocolate Hill, the work of the sharp-shooters, added to that of many small engagements, had further depleted our numbers 2,000 more at least. We had held our own under these harrowing circumstances from the last of April until August when the second division of 20,000 new Anzacs came to join us.

In the fleet of transports that bore the fresh contingent of Australians and New Zealanders, was the Southland she who was torpedoed in the Mediterranean. The men who arrived told us a most interesting story of the experience of the _Southland_ and the 1,300 troops aboard her. It will be recalled that after being torpedoed the _Southland_ had a remarkably long life. She was kept afloat for hours until beached on a rocky strand. The descriptions we got of the behaviour of the Anzacs and her crew were thrilling in the courage, cheerfulness and display of humour on the part of hundreds of Britishers, who had no way of knowing at what moment the wounded ship might plunge to the bottom of the sea.

One of the things they did was to hold an impromptu auction sale of the crippled Southland. Bids for the great boat, whose cost had been a half million, started at a shilling and while she was being battered on the sand and rocks, rose to the majestic sum of one pound. She was knocked down at that price to an Anzac, who later, in all hopefulness, was to file his claim of ownership with the marine registry at London. He announced his intention after the war of taking the Southland back home with him to make of it an Australian bungalow.

The Southland they told us landed with her nose high in the air, and there was rivalry as to who should be the last to leave the ship. Men scrambled up the steeply slanting deck, clinging to rails, cabin doors, and any other object offering hand- or foot-hold. There were big bathing parties around the wreck, before the men were picked up by the launches and barges from the other transports and battle ships. In the first of the shock from the torpedo and when all were in expectancy of the Southland's going down, the men assembled on the decks and bravely set up the Australian song composed by a British naval officer, which had become dear to them:

> "Gather around the banners of your country, Join in the chorus
> or the foam, On land or sea, wherever you be, Keep your eye
> on Germanee. England's home of beauty has no cause to fear,
> Should old acquaintance be forgot? No! No! No! No! No!
> Australia will be there, Australia will be there!"

8

IN THE TRENCHES

Letter of Lieutenant Colonel George Brenton Laurie, Commanding
Officer 1st Bn. Royal Irish Rifles

*N*ovember 25th, 1914. Back in the trenches, and very busy indeed, as apparently we intend to stay here for some time, and we are doing our best to make them habitable for the winter.

Our own dug-out, which was 3 feet deep, we have deepened to 4 feet, but just at this moment the roof beams of Major Baker's half have been carried away, whilst a sniper prevents our getting on the top of the roof to shovel off the earth and renew the beams.

Altogether a cheerful problem. However, like many others we shall gradually get this right. I was told that the Germans made a great attack in the afternoon two days ago on the Brigade to our right, but were beaten back. I have warned all my men to be ready for a rush at any time.

We made an amusing attack two nights ago with 8 men and one officer, all of whom were wrapped in sheets to avoid being seen in the snow. It took place from one of my trenches. The officer got to the German trench, where a man looked into his face. He fired his revolver at one yard, and his men following dashed forward and fired right and left down the trenches. A great scamper ensued, as you may imagine, and then from each German trench burst out a heavy rifle fire. Our guns were ready, and immediately opened on them in the darkness, and presumably caused the enemy many casualties.

I must say that I should never be surprised at the war coming to a sudden conclusion, or for it to last a very long time; but I fancy that a great deal depends upon the result of this battle in Poland.

The sniping gentleman is tremendously busy at present, but I hope he will not catch me on my way to luncheon. I have to go there very shortly. You see, I believe they have rifles fixed in clumps, and then they fire them by a sentry pulling a trigger. Of course, the shots are erratic to a certain extent, but they find out from spies where the general line of advance to our trenches is, scour them regularly, and now and then bag someone or other.

Last night passed quietly enough; we had our scrap about one o'clock. I was out, but nothing serious happened, I am glad to say. The weather has turned to rain again, and the country is losing the snow, whilst the trenches accumulate the rain and mud badly.

Please God this war will soon be over.

9

LETTER FROM THE WESTERN FRONT

2nd Lt Oswald Charles Blencowe - 26th Jan 1916.
18th Royal Fusiliers, B.E.F, France.

*M*y Dear Mother,
We are just out again and with any luck we shall not go in again for a month.

We have just done a month in and out of the trenches, this last time we were in for 9 days – 4 days in support & 5 days in the firing line. I wish I could tell you where it was but I shall only get the letter torn up by Old Man Censor!

Anyway, it was a very well known place and a very busy corner & I am glad to say I got through this time without having any more casualties in the platoon. It was really a most outstanding thing as the Company we believed had lost a good many in a place the Huns were only about 80 yards away and they were also holding a small crater in front of their lines the front edge of which was only about 35 or 40 yards distant from us. We were fairly safe from shells as the lines were so close together but there was a tremendous lot of sniping and any amount of rifle grenades flying about so one had to be most awfully careful. The best part of a rifle grenade is the fact that you can see it coming and it often lies on the ground for 5 or 6 seconds before it bursts so as a rule one has plenty of time to get round the nearest traverse.

At night its rather a strain on the nerves as one can't see them but can hear them coming quite plainly, the only thing to do is to stand absolutely still and listen for it to fall then after you have heard the thud of its fall – if its anywhere near – down you get as low as possible waiting for it to burst.

One afternoon one fell right into our trench but everyone saw it and nobody was hurt it blew a hole about 18 inches deep through the footboard! The second night we were in they sent about 80 rifle grenades at us before we spotted where they were coming from and then my rifle grenade men got started and the third we sent off did the trick, it landed right into the little crater where Old Hun was and apparently wiped them out as we weren't bothered again that night.

What impressed me more than anything was the sight of the country round us. Running right across our lines away into the German lines was a road – once a main road with trees each side and full of traffic and now – I can hardly describe it as one looked along it as dawn was breaking – every tree as far as one could see shot to pieces! Splintered trunks standing out against the skyline. Shell holes – broken stone work – torn barbed wire – equipment old and broken – dead Germans – rifles – absolutely despairing ruin everywhere so intense that one could almost touch it and tear ones feelings to shreds. I am afraid this sounds like Rosa N Carey at her worst but it made a tremendous impact on me and I shall never forget it. I wish some great artist or author could see it or feel it as I did and make it as a picture or article.

Must stop as it's getting awfully late. A loud smacker Dear little Ma I remain, your loving Oswald

He became a Sergeant in the Royal Fusiliers and in 1916 got his commission as 2nd Lieutenant in the Oxford & Bucks Light Infantry. He was killed on the 7th October 1916 at Guédécourt, France, when temporarily attached to the Rifle Brigade.

COLONEL A. C. MARTIN WRITES: 'He was my platoon sergeant all last winter on the La Bassée front... I had great admiration for his qualities and imperturbable character. All the officers of 'D' Company loved my Sergeant Blencowe. I shall never forget the picture of him after an hour's heavy bombardment of the piece of line his Platoon was holding. I went along to see what casualties and what damage had been caused and ran up against him looking the picture of robust health, unshaven (we had been in four days), and smoking an old pipe. He was so unexcited that he went on detailing a fatigue party or ration party without a word of comment although shells were still falling within 100 yards. He was always working loyally and most unselfishly for the comfort of the men and to help me.'

A brother officer writes: 'I am not writing in any official sense., but to express my admiration and appreciation for Blencowe. In the line he was of immense value to us and in the most trying hours, when things were as bad as shells and foul weather could make them, he showed that rare kind of cheerfulness which does not offend by its bumptiousness, nor depress by its artificiality. His spirits and efficiency were amazing. He set a high value on music and poetry. He sang well, and was strongly heard in the dug-out – carols, songs, choruses, old English songs, and Gilbert and Sullivan. One day we had returned from the trenches and gone back into a line of dug-outs. He pulled out the books he always carried with him, Omar Khayyam, and two volumes of the hundred best poems, and three of us lay awake, much longer than we could afford, reading aloud to one another. I know he was killed instantaneously. He was hit by a shell in the head when in front of his men, about ten yards from the enemy's line.'

LIFE IN THE TENCHES

Private G. Townsend, 2nd Battalion East Lancashire Regiment

When the rebellion broke out in South Africa we--the old "Lily Whites"--were the only imperial regiment kept in that country. We were sitting still and stiff for twenty days, till General Botha got his own troops ready. During that time we were guarding Cape Town, and it took us all we knew to hold in, because the big war was on, and we were about seven thousand miles away from the seat of it. We had to wait till General Botha was ready, and that was not for more than a month after the British and the Germans met in Belgium

We were eager to get away from South Africa, and at last we sailed-- but what a slow voyage it was! Almost a record, I should think. We were thirty-two days getting to Southampton; but that was because we had halts on the way and were convoyed by some of the British warships which have worked such marvels in this war. We had with us a noble cruiser which on a later day, though we thought her slow, knocked more speed out of herself than the builders ever dreamed of, and that was when she helped to sink the German warships off the Falkland Islands.

By the time we reached the south of England some big things had happened, and we were keener than ever to get to the front. We had not long to wait. We landed, and in less than a week we left England and crossed over to France, where we went into billets for four days, to settle down. From the billets we marched nearly seven miles and went into trenches. For three full months, in the worst time of a very bad year, I ate and drank, and slept and fought, in trenches, with intervals in billets, sometimes up to the hips in water and often enough sleeping on a thick couch of mud. I cannot go into too much detail, but I can say that our officers always tried to go one better than the Germans, for the sake of the men--and for the most part they succeeded. We have picked up a lot from the Germans in this trench game. They have a main trench and about four trenches behind that, the first of the four being about twenty yards away; so that if you knock them out of one you knock them into another.

That march to the trenches was a thing that can never be forgotten. It was very dark and raining heavily, so that we were thoroughly soaked; but we had no time to think of that, for we were bound for the firing line, we were going to fight for the first time, and we wondered who amongst us would be absent when the next roll was called. The trench to which we were bound was in its little way famous. It had been the scene of some terrible fighting. The Indian troops were holding it, but they had been driven out by the Germans, who took possession and thought they were going to hold it; but the Connaught Rangers made a desperate charge, routed the Germans with the bayonet and retook the trenches. The Connaughts won, but at a very heavy cost, and about 150 of the brave fellows fell and were buried near the little bit of sodden, muddy ground on which they had fought. It was to relieve the Connaughts that we went into the trenches on La Bassée Road that stormy night.

It was not a very cheerful beginning, and as much unlike going into action as anything you can imagine. But we felt queer, this being our first taste of fighting, as we slipped into the trenches with our rifles loaded and prepared to fire in the wild night at an enemy we could not see. As soon as we went into the trenches we were ankle-deep in mud, and we were in mud, day and night, for seventy-two hours without a break. That was the beginning of three solid months of a sort of animal life in trenches and dug-outs, with occasional breaks for the change and rest in billets without which it would not be possible to live.

In a storm-swept trench--a barricade trench we called it--pointing my rifle at an enemy I could not see, I fired my first shot in battle. My section of thirteen men was in the trench which was nearest to the Germans, and that meant that we were separated from them by only a very few dozen yards. An officer of the Connaughts had given a descriptive object to fire at, and this was a small white outhouse which could be dimly made out in the darkness. The outhouse had the German trenches just in front of it, and we made a target of the building in the hope of potting the men in the trenches.

The order came, one man up and one man down, which meant that a man who was firing was standing for two hours and the man who was down was sitting or otherwise resting, or observing, as we call it.

Throughout that long night we kept up fire from the trenches, all anxious for the day to break, so that we could see what sort of a place we were in and what we were doing; but when the melancholy morning broke there was nothing to see in front of us except the portholes of the German trenches.

We had got through the first night of battle safely and had given the Germans good-morning with what we came to call the "awaking fire," though it sent many a man to sleep for the last time--and we were settling down to make some tea. That was shortly after midday of our first day in the trenches. I was working "partners" with my left-hand man, Private Smith, who said, "I'll just have a look to see what's going on."

He popped his head over the top of the trench and almost instantly he fell into my arms, for he had been shot--there must have been a sniper waiting for him--and had received what proved to be a most extraordinary wound. A bullet had struck him on the side of the head, just below the ear, and gone clean through and out at the other side, leaving a hole on each side.

"I'm hit!" said Smith, as he fell--that was all.

I was badly upset, as this was the first man I had seen shot, and being my special chum it came home to me; but I didn't let that prevent me from doing my best for him. Smith was quite conscious, and a plucky chap, and he knew that there was nothing for it but to see it through till night came. We bandaged him up as best we could and he had to lie there, in the mud and water and misery, till it was dark, then he was able to walk away from the trench to the nearest first-aid station, where the doctor complimented him on his courage and told him what an extraordinary case it was and what a miraculous escape he had had. Later on Smith was invalided home.

During the whole of that first spell in trenches we had no water to drink except what we fetched from a natural trench half-a-mile away. Men volunteered for this duty, which was very dangerous, as it meant hurrying over open ground, and the man who was fetching the water was under fire all the time, both going and coming, if the Germans saw him. This job was usually carried out a little before daybreak, when there was just light enough for the man to see, and not enough for the Germans to spot him; and a chap was always thankful when he was safely back in the trench and under cover. At the end of the seventy-two hours we left the trenches. We came out at ten o'clock at night, expecting to be out for three days. We marched to an old barn which had been pretty well blown to pieces by shells, and into it we went; but it was no better than the trenches. The rain poured on to us through the shattered roof and it was bitterly cold, so that I could not sleep. We had everything on, so as to be ready for a call instantly, and without so much as a blanket I was thoroughly miserable. Instead of having three days off we were ordered to go into a fresh lot of trenches, and next afternoon we marched into them and there we stayed for six weeks, coming out seven or eight times. In these trenches we were in dug-outs, so that we got a change from standing sometimes hip-deep in mud and water by getting into the dug-out and resting there. A dug-out was simply a hole made in the side of the trench, high enough to be fairly dry and comfortable. During the whole of these six weeks it meant practically death to show yourself, and so merciless was the fire that for the whole of the time a dead German soldier was lying on the ground about a hundred yards away from us. He was there when we went and was still there when we left. We could not send out a party to bury him and the Germans themselves never troubled about the poor beggar. One day a chum of mine, named Tobin, was on the look-out when his rifle suddenly cracked, and he turned round and said, "I've hit one." And so he had, for he had knocked a German over not far away and no doubt killed him.

What with the weather and the mud and the constant firing we had a very bad time. Each night we had four hours' digging, which was excessively hard work, and if we were not digging we were fetching rations in for the company. These rations had to be fetched at night from carts three-quarters of a mile away, which was the nearest the drivers dare bring them. These expeditions were always interesting, because we never knew what we were going to get--sometimes it would be a fifty-pound tin of biscuits and sometimes a bag of letters or a lot of cigarettes, but whatever it was we took it to our dug-outs, just as animals take food to their holes, and the things were issued next morning.

One way and another we had between fifty and sixty men wounded in our own particular trenches, mostly by rifle fire, though occasionally a shell would burst near us and do a lot of mischief; and what was happening in our own trenches was taking place all around La Bassée. We should have suffered much more heavily if we had not been provided with periscopes, which have saved many a precious life and limb.

We paid very little attention to the German shell fire, and as for the "Jack Johnsons" we took them as much as a matter of course as we took our breakfast. Some of the German artillery fire actually amused us, and this was when they got their mortars to work. We could see the shot coming and often enough could dodge it, though frequently the great fat thing would drive into the ground and smother us with mud. For some of the German artillery fire we were really very thankful, because in their rage they were smashing up some farm buildings not far away from us. The cause of our gratitude was that this shelling saved us the trouble of cutting down and chopping firewood for warmth and cooking in the trenches. When night came we simply went to the farmhouse, and the firewood, in the shape of shattered doors and beams and furniture, was waiting for us. The farm people had left, so we were able to help ourselves to chickens, which we did, and a glorious change they were on the everlasting bully beef. A chicken doesn't go very far with hungry soldiers, and on one occasion we had a chicken apiece, and remarkably good they were too, roasted in the trenches. Another great time was when we caught a little pig at the farm and killed it and took it to the trenches, where we it.

When we had finished with the second lot of trenches we went into a third set, and I was there till I was wounded and sent home. These trenches were only about a hundred and twenty yards from the second lot, so that the whole of the three months I spent in trenches was passed in a very little area of ground, an experience which is so totally different from that of so many of our soldiers who were out at the war at the very beginning, and covered such great distances in marching from place to place and battle to battle. These chaps were lucky, because they got the change of scene and the excitement of big fighting, but the only change we had was in going out of one trench into another.

It was now the middle of December and bitter weather, but we were cheered up by the thought of Christmas, and found that things were getting much more lively than they had been. One night a splendid act was performed by Lieutenant Seckham, one of our platoon officers, and two of our privates, Cunningham and Harris.

An officer of the Royal Engineers had gone out to fix up some barbed wire entanglements in front of our trenches. The Germans were firing heavily at the time, and they must have either seen or heard the officer at work. They went for him and struck him down and there he lay in the open. To leave the trenches was a most perilous thing to do, but Mr. Seckham and the two men got out and on to the open ground, and bit by bit they made their way to the Engineer officer, got hold of him, and under a furious fire brought him right along and into our trench, and we gave a cheer which rang out in the night above the firing and told the Germans that their frantic efforts had failed. Mr. Seckham was a splendid officer in every way and we were greatly grieved when, not long afterwards, he was killed. Another of our fine young platoon officers, Lieutenant Townsend, has been killed since I came home.

We were so near the Germans at times that we could throw things at them and they could hurl things at us, and we both did, the things being little bombs, after the style of the old hand-grenade. We got up a bomb-throwing class and hurled our bombs; but it was not possible to throw them very far--only twenty-five yards or so. The West Yorkshires, who were near us, got a great many of these missiles thrown at them, but they did not all explode. One day a sergeant of ours--Jarvis--was out getting wood when he saw one of them lying on the ground. He picked it up and looked at it, then threw it down and instantly it exploded, and he had no fewer than forty-three wounds, mostly cuts, caused by the flying fragments, so that the bomb made a proper mess of him.

Our own bombs were made of ordinary pound jam tins, filled with explosive and so on, like a little shell, which, as the case of the sergeant showed, was not anything like as sweet a thing to get as jam.

The Germans were very fond of flinging these hand-bombs and seemed to have a great idea of their value in attacks and defence.

Christmas Eve was with us, Christmas Day was soon to dawn--and what a strange and terrible Christmas it was to be!

On Christmas Eve itself we plainly heard the Germans shouting. "A merry Christmas to you!" they said, and there was no mistaking the German voices that came to us in our trenches out of the darkness.

"A merry Christmas to you!"

Again the Germans greeted us, though we could not see them, and there was something pathetic in the words, which were shouted in a lull in the fighting. Some of our men answered the wish, but I did not--I had no heart to do so, when I knew that the message meant so little.

It may have been a matter of sentiment, because this was the time of peace on earth and goodwill towards men, or it may not; but at any rate the order came that if the Germans did not fire we were not to fire. But Christmas or no Christmas, and in spite of their greetings, the Germans went on firing, and we were forced to do the same, so throughout the night of Christmas Eve we had our rifles going and did not stop till it was daylight.

But the rifle fire was not the only sound of warfare that was heard--there was the sharp booming of artillery. The field batteries were hard at it and we knew they must be doing fearful mischief amongst the Germans. The night became truly awful; but how dreadful we did not know till Christmas Day itself, then, the firing having ceased, we saw that the ground in front of us, not very far away, was littered with the German dead.

A Merry Christmas!

The very men who had sent the greeting to us were lying dead within our sight, for the Germans had started to change their position and the British shells had shattered them. Something like two hundred and fifty of the Germans were lying dead upon the field, and sorry indeed must the dawn of Christmas Day have been to those who were left. Peace on earth!

There _was_ peace of a sort, for as we looked on the German dead from our trenches we saw two Germans appear in full view, holding up their hands, to show us that they were unarmed.

You can imagine what a solemn spectacle that was--what a Christmas Day it was which dawned upon us in the trenches. We knew instinctively what was wanted--the ground was littered with the German dead and the Germans wanted an armistice so that they could bury them.

One of our officers went out and talked with the two Germans who were holding up their hands--covered by British rifles. He soon learned what they wanted, and the armistice was granted.

It was about three o'clock in the afternoon of Christmas Day when the Germans set to work to bury their dead, and as they did so we left our trenches and stood on the open ground and watched them. We saw them perfectly clearly, because the main German trench was not more than 120 yards away, and the burial took place a few yards behind this.

I have seen a photograph of British and German soldiers fraternising on Christmas Day; but there was nothing of this sort with us. The only incident I witnessed was a British officer shaking hands with a German officer. That was all. I did not shake hands with them--and I had not the least wish to do so, though I bore them no ill-will on that sad Christmas Day.

I was thankful when Christmas was over and we had settled down to ordinary routine work, killing and being killed, for it is astonishing how soon you get accustomed to the business of firing on and being fired at.

The trenches had got from bad to worse. When I first went into them there was eighteen inches of water and five inches of mud; but now it was a matter of standing almost up to the waist in water. They became so bad that instead of using the communication trenches, which you might almost call tunnels, it was decided that we should cross the open country to get to our fighting-place, the main trench--indeed, we had no option, because the communication trench was almost impassable.

On a mid-January night, and very bad at that, we began the journey to the trenches. If there had been just ordinary honest darkness we should have been all right and quite satisfied; but though there was darkness enough there was plenty of light--the uncanny brightness which came from the star-shells.

Star-shells were going up all along the line and bursting. They are a sort of firework, giving a brilliant light, and as they exploded they showed us up almost as clearly as if we had been in daylight.

We had only a very short distance to go, but the star-lights made the journey to the trenches a desperate undertaking.

In single file, a little bunch of ten of us, crouching down, holding our loaded rifles and carrying all we possessed--we went along, losing no time.

From the stealthy way in which we started on our little trip you might have thought that we were burglars or villains bent on some fearsome job, instead of ordinary British soldiers getting back to their trenches.

We went with caution, and had not covered more than ten yards when what I take to be machine-gun fire was opened on us.

All at once, without the slightest warning, a real hail of bullets struck us, and of the ten men of us who were advancing in single file three were killed and four were wounded. The three who were shot down in the ghastly glare of the star-shells were ahead of me.

When that happened we were ordered to keep well apart and open out, but there was not much chance for those of us who were left; at any rate, no sooner had we obeyed and were making a little headway than I was struck myself on the head.

For half-an-hour or so I was unconscious; then I recovered and picked myself up and found that I was all alone. I crawled a few yards to a trench and got into it; but finding it full of water I thought I might as well be killed as drowned, so I got out, and not caring in the least for the German bullets or the star-shells, I made my way as best I could to the nearest dressing-station, and received attention. After that I found myself in a motor-car, and later at a clearing-station and on the boat for home.

You can see the scar of the wound here; but I don't bother about that. I suffer terribly from sleeplessness--and too often I see again the German soldiers who had wished us a merry Christmas--and were buried at the back of their trenches on the gloomy afternoon of Christmas Day.

WAR LETTER OF A PUBLIC SCHOOL BOY

Lieutenant Henry Paul Mainwaring Jones, Tank Corps
A letter to his brother

*H*ave you ever reflected on the fact that, despite the horrors of the war, it is at least a big thing? I mean to say that in it one is brought face to face with realities.

The follies, selfishness, luxury and general pettiness of the vile commercial sort of existence led by nine-tenths of the people of the world in peacetime are replaced in war by a savagery that is at least more honest and outspoken.

Look at it this way: in peace time one just lives one's own little life, engaged in trivialities, worrying about one's own comfort, about money matters, and all that sort of thing just living for one's own self. What a sordid life it is!

In war, on the other hand, even if you do get killed, you only antici-pate the inevitable by a few years in any case, and you have the satisfac-tion of knowing that you have "pegged out" in the attempt to help your country. You have, in fact, realised an ideal, which, as far as I can see, you very rarely do in ordinary life. The reason is that ordinary life runs on a commercial and selfish basis; if you want to "get on," as the saying is, you can't keep your hands clean.

Personally, I often rejoice that the war has come my way. It has made me realise what a petty thing life is. I think that the war has given to everyone a chance to "get out of himself," as I might say. Of course, the other side of the picture is bound to occur to the imagination. But there! I have never been one to take the more melancholy point of view when there's a silver lining to the cloud.

LIEUTENANT JONES WAS KILLED in action 31st of July 1917.

HIS COMMANDING OFFICER, in a letter Paul's family after his death, wrote:

"No officer of mine was more popular. He was efficient, very keen, and a most gallant gentleman. His crew loved him and would follow him anywhere. He did not know what fear was."

FROM THE CREW of his Tank:

"We all loved your son. He was the best officer in our company and never will be replaced by one like him."

A BROTHER OFFICER who served with Paul in the 2nd Cavalry Brigade, in paying homage to his character, wrote:

"He was a most interesting and lovable companion and friend. He never seemed to think of himself at all."

He was the very embodiment in himself of all that is best in the public-school spirit, the very incarnation of self-sacrifice and devotion.

A Dulwich Master.

THE BRITISH VICTORY AT NEUVE CHAPELLE

Sergeant William Gilliam, 1st Battalion Coldstream Guards.

*T*he battle of Neuve Chapelle began at half-past seven o'clock on the morning of March 10th, and ended at about half-past nine on the night of the 12th. Earlier on the morning of that famous day our battalion was ordered to stand to, as supports of the 1st Brigade.

We were told to be ready to turn out at ten minutes' notice; and we _were_ ready, for we were longing to have a settlement with the Germans, who had dug themselves in at Neuve Chapelle, and made themselves very comfortable and thought that no power on earth could drive them out. But we had a big surprise in store for them, and we sprung it on them like a thunderbolt when our massed guns roared soon after sunrise on that early day in March.

Whatever advantages the Germans might have had at the beginning of the war we had been getting the better of them, and we were certain that we were now much superior to the enemy in every way.

We knew that the British Army was becoming too much for them, and we were anxious to prove it that morning, when the biggest bombardment the world has ever known began, and along a tremendous front there came into action hundreds of the largest and the smallest guns that we had out in France.

I am sure that every man who was in at the beginning of this war, from Mons to the Marne and the Aisne, as I was, till I was invalided home wounded, will agree with me that there had been nothing like the British artillery fire at Neuve Chapelle. It was truly fearful. Something like five miles away, nearly five hundred British guns were bombarding the village, the batteries being on a front four or five miles in extent, so that there was only a few yards space between each gun. The result was that an immense wall of fire was seen where the artillery was in position, while the village itself was a target on which shells rained and made havoc. Nothing could withstand that awful cannonading--houses and buildings of every sort were shattered, and often enough a single shell was sufficient to destroy an entire house. When we got into the place at the end of the battle it looked as if some tremendous earthquake had upheaved it and thrown it down in a mass of wreckage. It was almost impossible to tell where the streets had been, and so enormous was the power of some of the shells that were fired and burst in the ground, that the very dead had been blown up from their resting-places in the churchyard, only to be re-buried by the falling walls around. The bombardment was bad enough for those who were out of it; for those who were in it the effect of the shell fire was paralysing. The Germans had had nothing like it, and more than one prisoner declared that it was not war, it was murder. We didn't quite see how they made that out; but it was near enough for the Germans, and we told them that we were only getting a bit of our own back for Mons. "And," we said, "this is only a taste of what's in store for you. It's nothing to what's coming!"

The roar of these massed guns was so deafening, and the noise of the exploding shells was so incessant, that we could not hear one another speak. The air was all of a quiver and you could see the heat in the atmosphere just as you see it when looking at the horizon in a tropical country, and as I saw it many times when we were in Egypt. The heat from the shells made the day for all the world like a hot summer day, and the fumes and flashes caused a strange mist that looked like rain, though the sun was shining.

The bombardment was grand and terrible beyond description; but there was one good thing about it, and that was that the Germans did not reply very often--they seemed numbed and stunned--and when they did, their fire was very slight and feeble, and so far as I could tell not one of their shells did any serious damage amongst the British forces. For half-an-hour the British artillery bombarded the enemy's first line of trenches, and this fire to the Germans must have seemed as if hell had been let loose, because everything that was in the line of fire was blown away or levelled to the ground--walls, trees, buildings, sandbags, even the barbed wire entanglements were carried away by shell splinters and shrapnel bullets, though unfortunately some of the entanglements escaped injury, and became death-traps for a number of our fine fellows who were hurling themselves upon the Germans.

Perhaps I should explain, so that my story is quite clear, that Neuve Chapelle, or what is left of it, stands on perfectly flat ground, with plenty of enclosed gardens and orchards and some wooded country near. The Germans had dug themselves into very complete trenches, and had built some strong breastworks near the highroad into which they had put a large number of machine-guns. In houses and elsewhere these weapons had been planted, and in some places they fairly bristled. Our object was to rout the Germans out of their trenches and houses and barricades, and in view of the deadly nature of machine-guns and rifles the work was bound to be long and heavy and costly. How desperate the assault was has been shown by the losses of some of our splendid line battalions.

When the bombardment of the first line of trenches was over, the way had been paved for the infantry, who were lying in their trenches, not far from the village. They were waiting eagerly for the order to advance, and when it came, they sprang out of their trenches with such shouts that you might have thought a lot of lunatics had been let loose. They dashed forward, and almost before it was possible to realise what had happened they were in the nearest German trench.

Then it was, even so soon after the battle had opened, that we knew how destructive the fire of our guns had been, for when the trench was reached there was hardly a German left to tackle. Our shells had landed plump into the enemy, and the result was that the trench was full of dead and wounded Germans. The few survivors did not hesitate to explain that they felt as if they could shake hands with themselves and to marvel that any one of them had come out of such a fire alive.

Our men were full of joy at such an ending to their rush, full of satisfaction to feel that they were making such a fine score, then came one of those misunderstandings and mishaps which are part and parcel of a fight in which the artillery cannot always see what it is doing--our own poor fellows suddenly found themselves under the fire of our gunners, who had started bombarding the trench again under the impression that it was still held by the Germans.

Imagine, if you can, what it meant to be in a trench like that, at such a time--a long narrow pit which had been knocked about by shells and was crowded with débris and killed and wounded men, and then to be under our own shell-fire. With unerring aim the shells came into the trench, causing consternation, and yet a sort of grim humour. Above the cries of the wounded and the shouts of the men came the loud voices of the officers, saying, "What is our artillery thinking of? What are they doing?" And at the same time doing their dead best to get their men out of it and back to their own trenches.

The order was now given to retire to our old position, and at last the order was carried out, but still some of our men were puzzled to know what had taken place, and they shouted, "What's wrong?" "What's happened?" and so on, while there were many cries for help and water. It was soon seen that there had been a mistake, and the best was made of it, though that was not much consolation for poor chaps who had been badly mauled and knocked about by fire that was meant for the enemy.

Noon came round on that first day of the battle and the chief thing we knew was that what we thought was finished had not been done, and we had to start afresh; but there was no grumbling or whining. It was realised that there had been a mistake, and it was taken in the way of British soldiers. And we were well rewarded, for suddenly our artillery re-started. They knew by this time what had happened, and I think they must have felt pretty savage, judging from the nature of their fire. We could see the destructive effects of it from our trenches, and it was a wonderful yet awful sight to watch the Germans being blown out of their trenches into the air, some of the bodies being shot twenty or thirty feet high. I am not going to dwell on the havoc that was caused amongst men; but you can imagine how dismembered parts were scattered by such a continuous bursting of shells.

The bombardment stopped abruptly, and in the strange calm that followed it we went off again, in just the same high spirits as before. This time we were lucky; there was no mishap, things went well and right, and by half-past two we had the joy and pride of knowing that we had made ourselves masters of the first line of the German trenches.

This line was piled up with the German dead, and the first thing we did was to get to work to clear some of the bodies away, so as to make a bit of room for ourselves to stand, keeping at the same time well under cover in case the enemy tried to get their own back; but they had been too badly shaken, and nothing of this sort took place. The Germans believed that Neuve Chapelle could not be taken, as it was so strongly fortified, and we now had a chance of seeing how much ground they had for their belief. A particularly strong defence was the barbed wire entanglements, which had been made uncommonly thick and complicated. This was the reason why even our destructive fire did not cut through the entanglements and why some of our infantry suffered so heavily. The Liverpool Regiment lost terribly, as so many of the officers and men were caught in the wires and had no chance of escaping from the fire which the Germans mercilessly directed upon them. The Liverpools were caught between the cross-fire of two German maxims as they tried to cut through the barbed wire, just in front of the German trenches. It was real heroism on the part of the Liverpools and it was a ghastly sight to see the brave fellows being cut down like flies.

In our captured trench, which was nothing more than a huge grave, we began, when we had made ourselves secure, to snatch a few mouthfuls of food; but we had no sooner started on this pleasant task than down came the order to prepare to advance.

"That's right!" the men shouted. "The music's started again! Let's get at the German pigs!"

Not very polite, perhaps, but in this war a good deal has been said on both sides about swine.

We sprang out of our trench and went full swing for the second trench--there were four trenches to storm and take before our object was accomplished. Very soon we were in amongst the Germans in the second trench, and it was a fine sight to see them being put through the mill.

Just in front of us, amongst the enemy, the shells from our own guns were bursting--a wonderful instance of the accuracy of modern artillery fire--and it was fascinating to see the shells sweeping every inch of the ground, and marvellous that human beings could exist in such a deadly area. Every now and then in would go one of the German parapets, and the almost inevitable accompaniment was the blowing into the air of limbs and mangled bodies. These things were not a laughing matter, yet often enough, as we watched a shell burst and cause havoc we laughed outright--which shows how soon even the most dreadful of happenings are taken as matters of course.

Now came the order for us to assault and away the infantry went, right into the German trench, with such a rush and power that the enemy seemed to have no chance of standing up against the onslaught.

The men of the Leicestershire Regiment hurled themselves into the thick of the bloody fray, not once, nor twice, but five times in succession did they rush the Germans with the bayonet--and at the end of that tremendous onslaught they had not a single German prisoner! Never while a German lives who survived the charges of the Leicesters will he forget what happened in the trenches at Neuve Chapelle--and what the Leicesters did was done by the Irish Guards. No prisoners--and no man who has been through the war from the start will blame them, for he knows what the Germans have done to our own brave fellows, not in fair fight, but when they have been lying helpless on the roadside, especially in the retreat from Mons.

The long and thrilling day was ending, darkness was falling, and we pulled ourselves together and prepared for a lively night. We fully expected a counter attack, but no--it seemed to be the other way about, for on our left we had our famous Gurkhas and Sikhs, and they were getting ready for work.

It was quite dark, about half-past nine, when suddenly there was a shout in the German trenches, and as it rose in the night a pair of our star-lights burst, like bright, beautiful fireworks in the sky, and showed us what was happening. It was this--the Indians had moved swiftly and silently in the night, they had crept and crawled up to the German position, and before the enemy knew what was taking place the heavy curved knife, which is the Gurkha's pride, was at work, and that is a weapon against which the German soldier, especially when in the trenches, seems to have no chance whatever. It is almost impossible to get over your surprise at the way in which these brave little Indians cover the ground in attacking. They crawl out of their trenches at night, lie flat on their stomachs, with the rifle and the bayonet in the right hand, and wriggle over the ground like a snake and with amazing speed. Having reached the enemy's trenches they drop the rifle and bayonet and out come the knives--and woe betide the Germans that are within reach. The Gurkhas are born fighters, the love of battle is in their very blood, and they fight all the more readily and gladly because they believe that if they are slain they are sure to go to heaven. If a German makes a lunge at him, the Gurkha seizes the bayonet with the left hand and gets to work with the knife. The plucky little chaps get their hands badly ripped with the German bayonets, and many came into Neuve Chapelle with half their left hands off.

The Germans hate the sight of these Indians, and those who could do so escaped from the trench. They lost no time in going--they fled, and no wonder, for they had suffered terribly, not only from the Indians, but also from the Black Watch, who had been at them with the bayonets. The Highlanders took a large number of prisoners; but the German dead were everywhere, and the trench was packed with them--indeed, all the trenches at the end of the battle were filled with Germans. During the 10th and 11th we made such good progress that we had taken three of the four trenches; then came the worst day of all, the 12th, for on that we were ordered to take the fourth trench which the Germans held. This was on the outskirts of the village and was strongly fortified. There was a strong blockhouse at the back of the trench which added greatly to the security of the position.

We were up and ready early--at half-past six--and as soon as day had broken the guns began their dreadful booming, and very solemn they sounded in the cold grey light, which is always so cheerless. The guns cleared the way again and did some excellent work in smashing away the wire entanglements and blowing up German works; then came the order to charge.

I was not in at the actual taking of this last trench, but I was lucky in being close enough to be able to see what was going on, and what I saw was some of the most furious fighting in the whole of the battle. The first charge was made with all the dash and courage of the infantry, who had already done so well. Our men rushed gallantly at the Germans; but so withering was the fire with which they were met and so hopeless seemed the obstacles that they were repulsed with heavy loss, and I know of nothing more heart-breaking to us who were watching than the sight of these soldiers being sacrificed and suffering as they did without, apparently, winning any success.

Again the artillery shelled the German position, then, across the ground which was littered with our dead and dying our brave fellows charged again. They sprang up from the shelter of their trenches, and with even greater fury than before threw themselves upon the enemy, only to be beaten back for the second time, by the cross fire of the machine-guns. In spite of all these losses and the awful odds against them our men kept their spirits up and vowed that they would still drive the enemy completely out of Neuve Chapelle, and get their own back for Mons and the rest of it, and so, while our artillery took up its tune again the men got a breather, and after a bombardment which lasted at least three-quarters of an hour there were shouts of

"Now, boys, again! Let 'em have it!"

And up the infantry sprang once more and dashed across the fatal ground. The men who were nearest to me were the 2nd Black Watch, and it did one's heart good to see the way the kilties swung towards the enemy's position. But it all seemed in vain, for at this point there was the blockhouse to be reckoned with. It was right in the centre and was a veritable little fortress which seemed a mass of flame and sent machine-gun and rifle bullets like hail. No troops could live or stand against such a fusillade, and so our men had to fall back even once more to the protection of the trenches.

By this time the position and danger of the blockhouse were known, and our artillery got the range of it, and that having been done, the end was merely a matter of time. A battery of British guns was trained on the blockhouse and the fire was so accurate that the fourth shell went through the left corner and the building was riddled with shrapnel and put out of action.

It was about this time that our fellows spotted an observation-post on the church in the village. As you know, churches and houses are objects that the British always avoid firing upon if they can, though the Germans have wantonly destroyed large numbers of both. There was the observation-post, plainly to be seen, and as the Germans were directing their artillery fire from it and the post was a danger and a nuisance to us and hindered our progress, a special effort was made to wipe it out. And the effort succeeded, for the British gunners got on it a "Little Harry," a shell that puts to shame even the Jack Johnsons and the Black Marias of the enemy. "Little Harry" settled the observation-post swiftly and finally, and then the fourth and last charge for Neuve Chapelle was made.

And what a charge it was! It was magnificent. Every bit of strength and courage that was left seemed to be put into it, and while the infantry dashed on with the bayonet and put the finish to the stubborn German resistance in the trenches and got the enemy fairly on the run, the Gurkhas and the famous Sikhs and Bengal Lancers hurled themselves on the flying regiments and cut them down with lance and sword.

It was a wonderful swirl of fighting. This time the blockhouse was stormed by the 2nd Middlesex and the Royal Irish Rifles.

All at once the guns had finished, and with wild cheers the old "Die-Hards" and the Irishmen rushed to the German trench and would not be driven back. By about half-past three the blockhouse was taken, and then it was seen that it had been defended by no fewer than half-a-dozen machine-guns and two trench mortars, to say nothing of rifles. These weapons and thousands of rounds of ammunition were captured and the Germans who had not been killed were found hiding under cover as best they could and they were thankful to surrender.

While this splendid piece of work was being finished our Indians on the left were doing heavy execution. The Bengal Lancers were driving the fleeing enemy straight through the village, if that could be called a village which was now an almost shapeless mass of burning and smoking ruins. And spies and snipers had to be searched for in the shattered buildings, while we had to leave the captured trenches for two reasons, because they were filled with dead and at any moment we might be blown out of them by mines which the Germans had laid. So we had to set to work, even while the fight was being finished, to construct new trenches, and we worked hard on these so as to make ourselves secure in case of a counter attack.

It was not long before we saw the victorious Indian cavalry returning. At about six o'clock we heard the thud of horses' hoofs, and looking up from the new trenches that we were making we saw the Bengal Lancers coming back from their pursuit and rout of the Germans. They had chased the enemy right through the village and into a big wood on the other side of Neuve Chapelle, and what they had done was shown by their reddened lances and the helmets and caps that were stuck on the steel. There were about six hundred of these fine horsemen and not one of them had less than "two trophies on his lance, while I saw one of them with no fewer than eight skewered on, and he was smiling all over his dark handsome face. So were the rest of them—they were all delighted with the success that had crowned their work, and we cheered them mightily and laughed too, for somehow we couldn't help doing both.

Meanwhile we were being shelled from a spot which we could not locate for some time, then we learned that the firing came from a fort on the left of the village which was known as Port Arthur. We were in the direct line of fire from it, and our position became very uncomfortable. The Germans who were in Port Arthur were a plucky and stubborn lot, for they refused to surrender when they were asked to do so, and declared that they would not cave in either for British or French or Russians. That showed a fine and right spirit, but at last these chaps had to stop, because our gunners got two or three "Little Harrys" into Port Arthur, and it came tumbling down about the defenders' ears.

It was now dark, past nine o'clock, and it seemed that the enemy was a long time making up his mind to attack us; but at about twenty minutes past the hour they began firing with their artillery. The very first shell they sent came right into my two sections of trenches, and killed one man and wounded half-a-dozen of us, including myself. The poor fellow who was killed had his head completely taken off his shoulders. I helped to bandage the other five before I troubled about myself. Then I looked around again and found that the Germans were well into the night attack; but they never got within fifty yards of our trenches.

What happened after that I am not able to tell you. I was sent to the field ambulance to have my wounds dressed, then I learned that I had got two shrapnel bullets in me, one in the left thigh and one on the other side, to keep it company.

In the ambulance train I went to Béthune, then on to Boulogne, then, on a Sunday afternoon—the 14th of March—I landed at an English Channel port and once again had experience of the care and kindness of friends and nurses in the hospitals at home.

For the second time I had been sent home wounded from the front. I was proud enough when I felt that I had tried to do my duty in the glorious rearguard fighting after Mons and in the battles of the Marne and Aisne; but I was prouder still to know that I had shared in the victory of Neuve Chapelle, in which we got our own back, with a lot of interest, from some of the finest troops of Germany."

PRISONER OF WAR GERMANY

Corporal Oliver H. Blaze, 1st Battalion Scots Guards

I hardly know where to begin my story, but perhaps I might start with a little tale of an air fight, because a night or two ago I happened to be in the streets when German airships raided London, and I could not help recalling the difficulty of hitting even a huge object like a Zeppelin in the night-time.

In the early days of September 1914, when we had got used to fighting, the battalion was on the march when a German aeroplane, decorated with two Iron Crosses, was sighted. At that time we were more than a thousand strong, and the lot of us opened fire with our rifles, rattling away with rapid fire, so that we soon accounted for about fifteen thousand rounds. At the same time another battalion not far away was on the job, so that a perfect fusillade was going on. The firing was tremendous, but it seemed as if the machine would not be touched. At last, however, the aeroplane was brought down, the observer being dead and the other man severely burnt and wounded. I do not know whether it was our battalion or the other which got the machine; but I called to mind the great difficulty of hitting an aircraft when I watched the raid on London. I was walking along, too pleasantly occupied to be thinking of war, and did not know of the affair until I reached a street corner and saw the people craning their necks skywards, watching the airship and the shells that were bursting under it.

Mons, Cambrai, the Marne and the like make an old, old story by this time, so I will get on to the tale of my nine months' captivity in Germany, as a prisoner of war.

It is common knowledge now that the Germans never lost a chance of trying to do something by treachery and trickery and not playing the game. Killed and wounded English soldiers were robbed of their coats by the Germans, who took them for their own use; and dressed in these coats the enemy on several occasions tried to get near us, to their heavy cost, when we got accustomed to the dodge.

One day, early in September, not long after we had gone out with the Expeditionary Force, a German machine-gun brigade came along, dressed in our uniform. We thought they were reinforcements, so we let them get very close and they occupied a ridge on our left. Ten minutes afterwards they opened fire on us; but our garrison artillery soon shifted them with sixty-pounders. The Germans killed a lot of the Coldstreams that day by this trick.

It was not long after this that we had one of those experiences which have been so often known in this great war. We were marching along in brigade column, with the Black Watch or Coldstreams, I am not sure which, leading. We were going through an area which had been reported all clear, and had got to a bend in the road, when the Germans started shelling us. It was one of those swift happenings which cannot be avoided in such a war as this, and before we fully realised what was taking place, a shell had burst and killed four stretcher-bearers of the Coldstreams, the N.C.O. who was in charge, and a wounded man who was being carried on a stretcher; and the same shell wounded a man in our front section of fours. That one shell did a fair lot of havoc, and it was quickly followed by several more; but these did not do much mischief.

What struck me most in this little affair was the coolness of our C.O., Colonel Lowther, now a brigadier-general. He personally conducted every company from the left of the road into a ditch on the right of the road.

"Keep cool, men," he said, "and come this way."

And we did keep cool, for the colonel took the direction of everything, in spite of the shelling, just as calmly as if he was carrying out a battalion parade at home--a really wonderful performance at a time like that, and one which completely steadied the lot of us, though we had got pretty well used to things.

But the Germans did not have a look in for long, for the Kilties got hold of the gunners and chased them off. I did not see much of it, except in the distance; but we heard the shouting as the Jocks got to work with their bayonets.

As we were going along the road we saw where the Germans had put out of action a whole battery of our artillery which was standing at the side of the road. The weather was dull and it started to drizzle, so that it was not easy to distinguish troops. While the battery was being knocked out some of our fellows--the Loyal North Lancashire, I think--were advancing across a field. To protect themselves from the rain they had covered themselves with their waterproof sheets. Seeing them, and not being able to tell who they were, but believing them to be Germans, our gunners opened fire on them; but what damage they did I don't know.

That was another of those things that will happen in war, and it could hardly be helped, for about this time it was a common dodge of the Germans to disguise themselves in British uniforms and attack us before we could tumble to the trick.

When we had crossed the Aisne and had got into the hills we had grown wary, and in crossing fields and open spaces we went in artillery formation, or "blobbing," as it is called. This "blobbing" was a splendid way of saving the lives of men when we were under fire, for it kept us in platoons closed, but 200 yards between each platoon, and so enabled us to escape a good many of the bursting shells.

We went along a whole stretch of country till we reached a small village and billeted there. In the morning we were on the move again, driving the Germans from one crest to another, but their position was too strong for us to shift them any farther, and then it was a long monotonous job of hanging on and waiting. They are practically in the same place now.

We did a lot of bayonet work from time to time; but I can't say much about it. I know that in one affair I saw a German. I stuck and he stuck-- and I don't remember any more--one goes insane. I got a bang on the back of the head from somebody, though I thought at the time that a stone had been thrown and had struck me. I remember that day well-- September 14th--because in addition to the charge I saw a Jack Johnson for the first time, though we christened them Black Marias and Coal-boxes then. This monster burst amongst some French Algerian troops, and shot a lot of them up into the air, literally blowing the poor devils to pieces.

On October 19th we marched away and moved by train, finally getting to Ypres. We dug trenches in a ditch on the night of the 22nd and occupied them, and on the morning of the 23rd I went on outpost duty, little dreaming of the fate that was in store for me. At that time shells were dropping very heavily between our line of trenches and a village not far away which was supposed to be occupied by the French.

It was about six o'clock in the morning when I went out with my patrol, of which I was corporal in charge. There were four of us alto-gether, and we were put on outpost duty in what proved to be a very warm corner. The shelling went on all day, and we were looking forward to our relief; but it did not happen to come, and so we had to hold on. The day passed and the night came, and it was not long after darkness that we knew that a strong rush was being made on us by the enemy--they proved to be the 213th Landwehr Battalion of Prussian Infantry.

I saw that we were being rushed, and I knew that our chance of escape was hopeless. I thought very swiftly just then, and my thought was, "We can't get away, so we may as well stick it. If we bolt we shall be shot in the back--and we might just as well be shot in the front; it looks better."

They were on us before we knew where we were, and to make matters worse, they rushed upon us from the direction of the village where we supposed the French to be.

There was a scrap, short and sweet, between our outpost and the Germans, and almost in the twinkling of an eye, it seemed, two of my men were killed, one got away, and I was wounded and captured.

A bullet struck me in the right arm and I fell down, and the Germans were on me before I knew what was happening. I still had my equipment on, and to this fact and the prompt kind act of a wounded German--let us be fair and say that not all Germans are brutes: there are a few exceptions--I owe my life, for as soon as I fell a Prussian rushed at me and made a drive with his bayonet. Just as he did so, a wounded German who was lying on the ground near me grabbed me and gave me a lug towards him. At this instant the bayonet jabbed at me and struck between the equipment and my wounded arm, just touching my side. The equipment and the wounded German's pull had prevented the bayonet from plunging plump into me and killing me on the spot, for the steel, driven with such force, would have gone clean through my chest. That was the sort of tonic to buck you up, and I didn't need a second prick to make me spring to my feet.

I jumped up, and had no sooner done so than a second bullet struck me on the wounded arm and made a fair mess of it, and I knew that this time I was properly bowled out.

I had fallen down again and was lying on the ground, bleeding badly;

and the next thing I knew was that I was being stripped. Everything I had on me, my equipment and my clothing, was taken away; not for the purpose of letting a doctor examine me, as one did later, but as part of a system of battlefield plunder which the Germans have organised.

The very first thing the doctor said when he saw the wounds was "Donnerwetter!" I was taken to a barn and left there till morning. I had treatment, then I was moved into another barn. The Germans were decent over the business, and there was no brutality or anything of that kind. I had been taken from the second barn, and was being carried across a field, when the ambulance was stopped by a German doctor who was on horseback. He looked at my arm, and instantly said that it would have to be amputated right away, as mortification had set in; and so, lying on the stretcher, which had been put down in the field, and round which a small green tarpaulin had been rigged to keep the wind and cold out, my arm was taken off. Injections had been made in the arm, and I felt no pain during the operation, which I watched with great interest. The doctor who performed it had studied at Guy's Hospital and spoke English well. When I had been removed to a German hospital in Belgium he saw me every morning, noon, and night, and I had exactly the same food as the Germans, while the old inspector of the hospital used to give me custard and fruit now and again, when he thought no one was looking; and I had cigarettes and cigars issued to me just the same as to their own men.

I was in this hospital in Belgium for a fortnight, and was then moved into Germany, being sent to Münster, in Westphalia, with a lot of wounded Germans. It seemed as if, in leaving Belgium, I had said good-bye to civilisation, in view of what happened during my imprisonment in Germany.

I very soon made acquaintance with German brutality to British prisoners of war--brutality and cowardice, of which I saw constant signs in my captivity; I say cowardice advisedly, because only a coward will hit and bully a man who can't hit back. On that point, however, there is some consolation. It was practically a death matter to strike a German soldier, even under great provocation; but if you were struck first, you had your remedy, and nothing pleased a British soldier more than to be struck, because that gave him his chance, and many a hard British fist got home on a fat German jowl. I shall always be thankful to know that I got one or two in on my own account, though I had only my left arm to work with. I did not, of course, strike until I had been struck first; but when I did hit out I got my own back, with a lot of interest.

That is getting off the track a bit, so I will go back. At Münster I was taken into a disused circus which had been turned into a hospital for prisoners, and when I got there the doctor examined my wound. It was all raw, but he messed about to that extent that I fainted. Two mornings afterwards--they only dressed us every two mornings--I was lying on a table, to be dressed. The job was to be done by a young German student, a born brute, for I tell only the plain truth when I say that he deliberately cut the flesh of my only arm with his lancet and scissors.

"English swine!" he said. "He's had one arm off, and he ought to have the other off, too!"

This was the type of fellow who was let loose on wounded helpless British prisoners of war. Those dressings were horrible experiences, as a rule, for I was held down on the table by German orderlies, who had about as much feeling and compassion as the table itself.

Let me give another illustration of the German way of treating wounded British soldiers. Just after Christmas I was moved into an open camp at Münster, and the only covering I had was a tarpaulin, the result being that I caught cold in my wound, and on January 2nd I was moved back into another hospital. I knew nothing whatever about the regulations of the place, so that I saw nothing wrong in walking along an ordinary looking passage. As I did this there came towards me a man who corresponds in rank to our regimental sergeant-major. I was suffering greatly from my stump, and was quite helpless; yet this fellow seized me by the scruff of the neck and the seat of the trousers and threw me out of the passage--and it was not till later that I learned that the passage led to the operating-room, and that patients were not allowed to use it. Such a thing could not possibly happen in a British military hospital containing wounded German soldiers. It is only fair to say that the food we got in hospital was good.

Though my wound was not healed, I was sent away from the hospital and back to the camp. That was bad in some ways, but it had a fine compensation, for I was attended by two of our own medical officers of the Royal Army Medical Corps who were also prisoners-- Captain Rose and Captain Croker. I believe they have been exchanged now. I need not say what a joy it was to be looked after by our own splendid doctors, after my experience of German brutality and callousness.

GERMAN HATRED AND TREACHERY

Corporal William David Bratby, 2nd Battalion Middlesex Regiment

*T*he old "Die-Hards" went into action at Mons nearly a thousand strong; but when, after Mons had been left behind, a roaring furnace, the roll was called, not more than 270 of us were left. D Company came out a shattered remnant—only thirty-six men, and no officers. When what was left of us marched away, other regiments were shouting, "Three cheers for the Die-Hards!" And three rousing cheers they gave; but I had no heart for them, because I had left my younger brother Jack, a "Die-Hard" like myself. They told me that he had been killed by a bursting shell while doing his duty with the machine-gun section.

I did not say much. I asked the adjutant if any of the machine-gun section had returned, and he answered sadly, "No, they've all gone."

Jack and I were brothers and had been good old chums all our lives —I had taught him a bit of boxing and he was most promising with the gloves, and we had a widowed mother to keep; so I really felt as if something had gone snap in my head and that all I cared for was to get my revenge from the Germans. The last words I heard him say were, "Well, Bill, I'm going right into the firing line," and I remember laughing and saying, "Yes, Jack, but you're not the only one who's going to do that."

Jack laughed too and said, "All right, Bill, I'll see you in the firing line," and with that he went and I saw no more of him.

I had been in the regiment five years and nine months when the war broke out and Jack had served more than two years. I had become a corporal and he was a lance-corporal.

The days in the beginning were swelteringly hot; but the "Die-Hards," being typical Cockneys, made the best of them. Our Brigade consisted of ourselves (the 4th Middlesex), the 2nd Royal Scots, the 1st Gordon Highlanders and the 2nd Royal Irish Rifles. We began operations with trench digging, one particular trench, the machine-gun trench, being allotted to B Company. I helped to superintend the construction of the trenches, and I was proud of the work when I saw what was done from them when the Germans showed themselves.

Our machine-gun caused enormous havoc amongst the German ranks, and I am sure that my brother did his part in settling a lot of them, for he was keen on his work and full of go. The Royal Irish at this stage were doing splendidly—they were not more than 350 yards from the enemy, separated from them by a railway—and they were lucky enough to fetch one gun out of action again, but the enormously superior numbers of the Germans told and the famous retreat began. The machine-gunners had suffered very heavily and it was hard to learn anything definite about the position in the trenches.

Officers and men were falling everywhere on both sides, and I saw a reconnoitring patrol of Uhlans bowled over in trying to avoid some of the 4th Royal Fusiliers. An officer and seven men of the Uhlans were killed in that little affair without getting in a shot in return. It was not much, but it was something cheering after what we had gone through at Mons. We looked upon it as a bit of sport, and after that we went into châteaux, cafés and other places, and discussed affairs in a proper Tommy-like spirit. It is very strange, but if it had not been for the language I could have thought at times that I was back in Kilburn or in London, on strike duty again, as I was at the time of the railway trouble three years ago.

We were fighting a rearguard action for three days right off the reel, and doing that wonderful march to which "Kitchener's test" or anything like it was a mere nothing. Owing to the heat, we discarded overcoats, kits and in some cases rifles and equipment. Our transport was blown to pieces three days after Mons, which to the 8th Brigade is known as *the* Wednesday.

But lost kit and shattered transport mattered little to most of us, and certainly had slight significance for me, because the only thing I had in mind was this determination to get revenge. I am not exaggerating in the least, I am merely putting down on record the state of my feelings and wishing to make you understand how remarkable a change had come over me, an alteration such as is brought about, I take it, by war, and war alone. Perhaps, too, the excessive stress and strain of those early days of the war had something to do with my condition; but whatever the cause, there it was. Danger itself meant nothing, and I, like the rest of us, took the ordinary fighting and the incessant and truly horrible shell fire as a matter of course, a part of the day's work. I bided my time, and it came.

We had crossed the Aisne, a dangerous unit still, in spite of our losses, for we had received reinforcements from the base; but just before crossing the river we sat down on the road, waiting for a favourable opportunity to cross by a pontoon bridge which the Engineers were building. That pontoon replaced a bridge which had been blown up.

On the word "Rise" we fell in, and in doing so a man had the misfortune to shoot himself through the hand.

The colonel came up at once and ordered the injured man to go back to the hospital in a village about a mile and a half up the road, in rear of the bridge. I was told off to take him, and we went to a house that had been turned into a hospital, the people in it being typically French. There were some sad cases there, amongst them one of our own fellows who had been severely wounded and a trooper of the 4th Hussars who was the only survivor of a reconnoitring party. He had been shot while going through the village that morning. Just at that time we had had many losses of small bodies—in one case a sergeant and five men had been blown to pieces.

After I had got the wounded man into the hospital I asked the "monsieur" in charge of the house for some tea, which he very willingly produced—it had no milk in it, of course, but by that time I had almost forgotten that milk existed.

At this time the village was being shelled, but that did not affect the enjoyment of my tea-drinking, and after that refreshing draught and a chunk of "bully" and some biscuit crumbs which I found in the corner of a none-too-clean haversack, I "packed down" for the night.

At about four o'clock next morning I awoke and went back to the bridge, which my battalion had crossed on the previous day, the "Diehards" being the first to have the honour to cross. By this time we had got past the sweltering stage of things and had become accustomed to soaking weather, and on this particular morning I was thoroughly cold and wet and generally "fed up" with things; but I still glowed with the longing to get level with the Germans.

You must bear in mind that regiments had been broken up and scattered in the most astonishing manner and had become mixed up with other regiments, and I had lost my own and had to set to work to find it.

I got over the bridge and reached some artillery.

"Have you seen anything of the Middlesex?" I asked.

"Yes," the gunners answered, "they've just gone into action on the brow of the hill."

I made my way towards the top of a neighbouring hill and found that my battalion had taken up a position there, but I had to wander about aimlessly, and I did so till I came across one or two men who were separated from the battalion. They directed me to the actual position, which was on the ridge of the hill, and to the ridge I went and found that it was lined with remnants of the brigade.

I tried to find my own company, but could not do so, as it had been surprised in the night; so I attached myself to another and lay down with the corporal on the sodden ground.

Wet through, cold, hungry and physically miserable, but still tough in spirit, we lay there, wishing that all sorts of impossible things would happen.

The corporal showed me where he had hit a German scout. We watched the poor devil rolling about—then we finished him off.

In addition to the wet there was a fog, and under cover of this the Germans crept up and were on us almost before we knew of their presence.

The alarm was first given by a man near us who was suffering from ague or some such ailment and had been moaning and groaning a good deal.

Suddenly he cried, "Here they are, corporal! Fire at 'em!"

My loaded rifle was lying just in front of me. I snatched it up, and as I did so the Germans jumped out of the mist on to us, with loud shouts. I brought the first German down and my chum dropped one; and we managed to fetch the officer down. He was carrying a revolver and a stick, like most German officers, so that you had no difficulty in distinguishing them.

When the alarm was given I gave a quick look over a small hump in the ground and then we were rushed; but I hated the idea of retiring, and kept on shouting, "Crawl back! Crawl back!"

Machine-guns and rifles were rattling and men were shouting and cursing. In the midst of it all I was sane enough to hang on to my fire till I got a good chance—and I did not wait for nothing.

Up came two Germans with a stretcher. They advanced till they were not more than twenty-five yards away, for I could see their faces quite clearly; then I took aim, and down went one of the pair and "bang" off the stretcher fell a maxim. The second German seemed to hesitate, but before he could pull himself together he had gone down too. I began to feel satisfied.

By this time the order to retire had been given and I kept on shouting, "Keep down! Crawl back!" and the lads crawled and jumped with curious laughs and curses.

In that excited retirement the man who was with me was shot in the chest. I halted for a little while to see what had really happened to him, and finding that he was killed I took his waterproof sheet and left him. I hurried on until I was in a valley, well away from the ridge; then an officer managed to get us together and lead us into a wood.

As we got into the wood I spotted a quarry. I said to the officer, "Is it best to go down here, sir?"

"I'll have a look—yes," he answered.

We went into the quarry, where there were Royal Scots, Middlesex, Gordons and Royal Irish.

The officer was afraid that we might be rushed, in which case we should be cut up, so he put a man out on scout. We were not rushed, however, and when the firing ceased we filed out and lined the ridge again, and there we lay, expecting the Germans to come back, but for the time being we saw no more of them.

By some means one of the Irishmen had got drunk and wanted to fight the Germans "on his own." He was shouting for them to come on and was wandering about. Soon afterwards he was found lying on the top of the hill, having been shot in the thigh. He was carried out of action and I have never heard of him since.

After that affair of the hill-crest we had a lot of trench work, and very harassing it was. For five days we stayed in trenches, so near to the enemy that it was death to show your head.

Trench fighting is one of the most terrible features of the war, for not only is there the constant peril of instant death, which, of course, every soldier gets accustomed to, but there is also the extreme discomfort and danger of illness arising from insanitary surroundings. Often enough, too, when a new trench was being dug we would find that we were working on ground that had been previously occupied, and the spades brought up many a ghastly reminder of an earlier fight.

Sometimes in this wonderful warfare we were so very close to the Germans that when we sang hymns—and many a hymn that a soldier has sung at his mother's knee has gone up from the trenches from many a brave lad who has given his life for his country—the Germans would harmonise with them. It was strange to hear these men singing like that and to bear in mind that they were the soldiers who had done such monstrous things as we saw during the retreat, when they thought that certain victory was theirs. Time after time, with my own eyes, I saw evidence of the brutal outrages of the German troops, especially on women and children, yet it seems hard to convince some of the people at home that these things have been done.

At one time in the trenches, for a whole week, we were so situated that we dare not even speak for fear of revealing our position—we were subjected to an enfilade fire and did not dare to speak or light a fire, which meant that we had no hot food for a week, and we could not even smoke, which was the biggest hardship of all for a lot of the lads. We were thankful when we were relieved; but were sorry indeed to find how dearly the newcomers paid for their experience. We had been cramped and uncomfortable, but pretty safe, and the Germans had not been able to get at us to do us any real mischief, but our reliefs walked about as unconcernedly as if they were on furlough, with the result that on the very first night they went into action they lost a hundred men.

The system of trenches grew into a sort of enormous gridiron, and if you walked about—which you could only attempt to do at night—you were almost certain to drop into a trench or a hole of some sort. This made getting about a very exciting job, and it added enormously to the intense strain of fighting in the trenches, a strain which was hardest to bear in the night-time, when we were constantly expecting attacks and when the Germans adopted all kinds of devices to get at us.

The Germans are what we call dirty fighters, and they will take advantage of anything to try and score over you. They have no respect for anything and made a particular point in many of the places they overran of desecrating the churches. They never hesitated to turn a place of worship into a scene for an orgy, and I remember going into one church after the Germans had occupied it and being shocked at their conduct. In this particular place they had been able to lay hands on a good deal of champagne and they had drunk to excess, turning the church into a drinking-place, so that when we reached it there was an indescribable scene—filthy straw on the floor, empty champagne bottles littered everywhere, and the whole building degraded and desecrated.

The Germans had got a French uniform and stuffed it with straw and propped it up to resemble a man, and on the uniform they had stuck a piece of paper with some writing on it in German. I do not know what the writing was, but I took it to be some insult to the brave men who were defending their country and preventing the Germans from getting anywhere near Paris. I could tell you much more and many things of the Germans' dirty fighting, and of things that were far worse than such an incident as turning a church into a drinking-place; but perhaps enough has been said on that point of late.

But that dirty fighting does not mean that the Germans do not fight bravely—far from it; they are hard cases, especially when they are in overwhelming numbers, which is the form of fighting that they like best of all. They are great believers in weight and hurling masses of men at a given point, and they are absolutely mad at times when their opponents are the English.

I will tell you of a case which illustrates this particular hatred. One night we were attacked by the Germans, though there was but little hope of them doing anything serious, in view of the fact that we were in trenches and that there were the barbed wire entanglements every-where. There had been no sign of an attack, but in the middle of the night a furious assault was made upon us and a young German by some extraordinary means managed to get through the entanglements. An officer of the Buffs was near us, and in some way which I cannot explain the German managed to reach him. With a fierce cry he sprang directly at the officer, put an arm round his neck, and with the revolver which he held in the other hand shot him.

It was the work of a moment; but it succeeded—so did our bayonet attack on the German, for almost as soon as his shot had rung out in the night a dozen bayonets had pierced him. He died very quickly, but not before he had managed to show how intensely he hated all the English. He was a fine young fellow, not more than seventeen or eighteen years old, and it was impossible not to admire the courage and cleverness he had shown in getting through the awful barbed wire entanglements and hurling himself upon us in the trenches in the middle of the night. The point that puzzles me even now, when I recall the incident, is how the young German managed to make such a clean jump for the officer. I daresay there was something more than luck in it.

At this time we were with the Buffs, who told us that they were being badly troubled by snipers. I was in a trench with Lieutenant Cole, who was afterwards killed, and he said to me, "Corporal, the snipers are worrying our people, but it's very difficult to locate them. Try and see what you can make out of it."

It was very difficult, but I set to work to try and make something out. Before long, with the help of the glasses, I concluded that the sniping came from a wood not far away, and I told the officer that I thought they were in a tree there. The consequence was that a platoon loaded up, went round, concentrated their fire on this particular spot and brought down two German roosters from a tree. We were glad to be rid of the pests, and they ought to have been satisfied, for they had had a very good innings.

I have been telling about the determination I had to be revenged for my brother's death. That was my great object, and I kept it in mind before anything else—and I think I carried it out. Apart from any motive, it is the British soldier's duty to do everything he can to settle the enemy, especially the Germans, and I am glad that I did my bit in this respect.

Now listen to what has really happened. After all that fighting and suffering with the grand old "Die-Hards" I got my own turn, after many wonderful escapes. A shell burst near me and the fragments peppered me on the right hand here and about this side of the body, and bowled me out for the time being. I was sent home, and here I am in London again, getting well and expecting the call to come at any time to go back to the front. When it comes I shall be ready to obey.

Look at this postcard. It is written, as you see, by a British soldier who is a prisoner of war in Germany, and it tells the glad news that my brother, who, I was told, was killed months ago by a bursting shell, is not dead, but is alive and well, although he is a prisoner of war.

ABOUT THE EDITOR

Kevin Gorman served in the British Army for twenty five years. He read history at Birkbeck College, University of London and has a Masters Degree in Intelligence and Security Studies from Brunel, London University. He currently works in the City of London

NOTES

1. Wood, W, (Ed), *Soldiers Stories' of the War*, Chapman & Hal, London 1915, page 29.

2. Anonymous, *Letters from a Soldier of France 1914-1915: Wartime Letters from France*, 1917.

3. Ogilvie, FB, *Stories and Letters From the Trenches: Three Months in the Trenches*, New York, 1915.

4. Ditto, Private McGlade.

5.Wood, W, (Ed), *Soldiers Stories' of the War*, London 1915, page 41.

6. Capart, G P, Drouillard, JC, (Ed), *A Blue Devil of France: Epic Figures and Stories of the Great War, 1914-1918*, New York, 1918.

7. Wood, W, (Ed), *Soldiers Stories' of the War*, Chapman & Hal London 1915, page 54.

8. Fallon, Captain, D, *THE BIG FIGHT. (Gallipoli to the Somme,)* New York, 1918.

9. Vere-Laurie, F, (Ed), *Letters of Lieut-Colonel George Brenton Laurie*, Gale & Polden, Ltd, Aldershot, 1921.

10. Doug R, *1916 Brought into Perspective*, www.europeana.eu

11. Wood, W, (Ed), *Soldiers Stories' of the War*, Chapman & Hal London 1915, page 94.

12. Housman, L, (Ed), *War Letters of Fallen Englishmen,* New York, 1930.

13. Wood, W, (Ed), *Soldiers Stories' of the War,* Chapman & Hal London 1915, page 291.

14. Wood, W, (Ed) *In The Line of Battle,* Chapman & Hall, London 1916.

15. Wood, W, (Ed), *Soldiers Stories' of the War,* Chapman & Hal London 1915, page 82.

Printed in Great Britain
by Amazon